VALENTINA MICHAILOVNA KOPYTINA

from Stalin to Auschwitz, Rescue & New Identity,
Trained for a German War Nurse, USA

To Frank & Penny

Glenda M French

GLENDA M. FRENCH, MSW

outskirts
press

This memoir did not begin with the idea of publication. It could have accurately been called *Tea and Cookies with Vallie*, as it truly was over tea and cookies that her stories began to emerge and continued to be told over a period of about 2 years.

I was a recently retired 60-year-old clinical social worker who had a practice of psychotherapy for 20 years. Vallie was 80 at the time and had a heart full of memories, very few of which had been shared with anyone. In my recent retirement, I missed hearing the stories and challenges of my clients' lives. Vallie had stories needing to be told. Neither of us knew in the beginning how much our needs would meet through this friendship.

Her stories came at first as facts that most people who knew her were already aware of, such as she was from the Ukraine region of Russia and came to America after World War II.

As she began to trust me, she told stories that hurt her so much that it was as though the telling itself was like ripping a bandage off an old wound and finding it still bleeding and infected. She gradually began to trust me with her stories and her tears. I just listened. I hoped and prayed this telling and these tears would be cleansing to her wounded spirit.

I had not written down anything she told me until one day as she was telling a story. Writing was my own way of coping with what I had heard but could not share with anyone else. As I put this story onto paper, I was able to get it out of my emotions and mind, at least for a little while. I knew I did not have to think about it. I could, if I wanted, go back and read it again . . . or just destroy it.

One day, she began to tell this story again but with more detail. This can happen as memory begins to return. So when I innocently mentioned that when I had written this story down the first time she told me, there was instantly a furrow between her eyebrows and worry in her voice. She wanted to know why.

"Did anyone else read it?"

"No," I told her. "It was only because I found it so interesting, and I didn't want to forget it. It's just something I like to do."

Because she is a consummate caretaker, the professional side of me did not want to contaminate her stories by a concern she would have to protect me. She wanted to read it, so I took a copy to her. I had no idea at this time how much fear still lived inside her. She read it and cried while I sat watching.

"I like the way you write," she said. "It doesn't make me sound stupid, and you seem to say the truth even more than I could say it."

"That's what I call 'listening below the words.' But is it accurate?"

"Oh yes, honey."

I don't know when or how we agreed to continue the process of her telling the stories and me writing them down. It just evolved. The stories did not come in any order. She told stories as the memories began to return to her. She did not talk about this early part of her life every time we were together.

After a couple of years of piecing the story together, she wanted it to be over. She wanted to find the gaps in the story and fill them in so we could be finished and do something much more fun. It was as though she had drained out a clogged sewage pipe of memory. She was feeling cleaner, safer (a little), and the nightmares of 60 years seemed to be gone. Newer memories began to come—fun, happy, loving memories of her life in Russia that had been obliterated by so complete an avoidance of the past.

Glenda French
November 7, 2009

Acknowledgments

First and foremost, my appreciation goes to Vallie for her confidence that I could tell her story.

Dr. C. Carter Boggs, MD my companion for loving me and believing in me every step of the way.

My daughters Julia Cameron, Medora Cesarano, and Maria Buschbach whose love has always inspired and motivated me. To their father, Robert French for editing assistance and encouragements to keep at it.

My friend Sandy Helmic for lots of emotional and practical assistance.

Finally, to Jamie Rath and Amy Belt at Outskirts Press for guiding me through the publishing process.

December 2008

It was a snowy day in the Pacific Northwest, Portland, Oregon. I was cross-country skiing down the hill by her house and decided I would stop by to see how she and her frail, elderly husband were doing.

"Oh, Glenda, Glenda. I'm so glad you came." She was bouncing up and down, all five feet of her, with sparkling, clear blue eyes, and a smile about to jump off her face, she was so excited.

"This morning about 7:30, my phone rang. A woman was talking so clearly, that it could have been you.

"The woman asked, 'Is this Valentina Michauloina Kopytina?' and I thought, 'Who is this woman? I know that name.'

"Honey, that was so crazy, but see, in Russia, they would call me by my complete first name and my father's last name. You do that out of respect. And I knew that name was familiar, but I don't hear it anymore. It's my Russian name."

Table of Contents

CHAPTER **1**

The Beginning and
The Background

I WAS BORN July 8, 1926, in Kiev, Russia. A blue baby. Mama was 21 years old, and Papa was 26. Stalin had been in power 8 years following the death of Lenin. He was a wolf in sheep's clothing. We learned only after the war that Stalin was responsible for the death of 20 million of his own people by deliberate starvation.

People were terrified of him but could and would never show it. He created a society where no one trusted anyone else. There was no innocence even in casual conversation. Something could be misunderstood that would put you or your family in jeopardy. The next thing you would know is that someone had "disappeared."

When he took power in 1918, he began to redo the entire country. For example, my maternal grandparents had owned a house and an ink factory. Stalin took control of both. No one could own anything privately. When I was born, my parents lived in one small room in a house that had once belonged to a family. A great depression was going on when I was born, and it had been going on for many years. People were hungry and fearful. Millions were dying in Ukraine, the breadbasket of the Soviet Union.

Other things about the world I was born into: My grandparents had been religious people and practicing members of the Russian

Orthodox Church. But during Stalin's reign, you could be punished if you were caught possessing a Bible or were heard even mentioning the name of God. Formal religious practice no longer existed. Stalin was to be the only superior being we were supposed to depend upon. He was to be our "Father," our "Papa." His picture had to be hanging in the house because you never knew when someone would come into your house to make sure it was hanging there. Stalin was a papa who was feared, especially if you were not willing to join the Communist Party. My true Papa would not join.

Here's a little more about the world I was born into in 1926.

I was told from my earliest memories that I was a "blue baby." I know now that this is a congenital heart condition that causes the blood not to get enough oxygen, so the skin takes on a "blue" look from the poorly oxygenated blood. I wasn't supposed to be able to live. I learned this as I got older. My maternal grandmother had been or was a religious woman, a believer in God. She had to hide this, of course, or risk punishment. So when I was born with little chance of living, she called for a priest. I guess that would be the name. But I was only told that someone came to the house and said prayers over me so that when I died, I would go to the right place. But you know what is strange? I wanted to see this man and thank him for saving my life. I had a picture of him in my mind. He had black hair, a long, black beard, and wore a long, black coat. Where did I get that image?

Glenda: Sounds like Rasputin or an Orthodox priest.

I guess. Maybe I just had seen pictures or had been told what a priest looked like. Grandma also told me that Mama and Papa were so upset. You know, at that time, and I think still today in Russia, educated people such as my parents only had one or sometimes two children. It was all you could take care of. People who lived in the country might have even 14 children, but they lived off the land, so the parents could support them easier. Also, Stalin had said, "The more children you have, I'll give you help." So I'm sure that encouraged families to have all those kids. Others, such as my parents didn't believe him.

Mama and Papa Meet

I've been thinking about Mama and Papa, and I want to talk about something sweet today. I always loved the story about how they met. I had them tell it to me many times. Mama worked for a newspaper, and Papa was in school at the university. He was studying to become an architect and engineer. This part of Kiev had a river, and Mama lived on the level of the river. Papa lived at the top of a very steep cliff above the Dnieper River.

Mama worked in the basement of the building on the level of the Dnieper where the printing machines were, and the basement had a window well making the actual window below the sidewalk level. Papa had to walk past that window on his way to and from the university to get to the corner where he caught his bus.

One day while walking past, he looked down and saw the most beautiful head of long, blond hair. So every time he walked past, he wanted to see the face of the woman with the beautiful hair. But she was never looked up when he passed, so he decided on the next trip, he would kick a little pebble at the window.

The next day, she was standing there working, facing the window with her head down. He kicked a pebble at the window, and the woman looked up. With a big smile on his face, he would always say, "That's when I saw that beautiful face and those blue eyes."

He didn't know when she got off work; so he would walk to the corner bus stop and just stand there hoping she too would come to catch the bus. He didn't know that Mama lived down by the river and never took the bus home. Finally, one day, his patience paid off, and she arrived at the bus stop. He introduced himself, and as they say, the rest is history.

Mama

My mama was so beautiful. I remember as a little girl asking a woman, "Am I right to think my mama is so beautiful? Do I just think she is so beautiful because she is my mama?" And this woman said, "Your mama is so very beautiful, and your papa so handsome. And if I weren't already married, I would be interested in your papa." That scared me. I didn't want her to see my papa ever again.

Mama could cook and bake and make her own patterns for sewing, and she would draw pictures to embroider onto clothes. And, remember, this was all during a time of depression in the country, so you had to make do with what you had. Because Papa wouldn't join the Communist Party, we did not have a card. If you did not have this card saying you were a member of the party, you could not shop at the places that had more food or cloth—whatever you needed.

I think that some of my relatives tried to bring extra food to us as they had chosen to join the party. I remember Mama wanted Papa to join so we would be able to buy more.

I also remember one time I had a bad infection under a fingernail. Mama knew how to fix up a concoction from an aloe plant and wrap the finger. It had been very painful, and she made it well. She was so smart in my eyes, and I loved her for how she took care of me.

Every day when I came home from school, I couldn't wait to get close enough to look up to that third-floor window where I would see Mama waving and smiling at me. We were very poor. Same as most people. But when I came home, we would have tea and a special treat and talk about my day. She would take an old, dry piece of bread, cut it into four pieces, dip it in a little sugar, and warm it on the skillet. That tasted as good as any cookie ever did.

Mama came to all my school shows. I would see her looking at me with such pride and a big smile and tears in her eyes.

The Water Fountain

Mama had taught me never ever to drink water from the water fountain in the park. She said there were germs in it, and I might get a disease from the fountain. She taught me to cup my hand and get the water in it and drink from my own hand. One day, I was outside playing with my friend Olga. We were having such fun. I became very thirsty and wanted a drink. I didn't want to run into the house, so I looked around to see if anyone who knew me was watching. Not seeing anyone, I leaned over and took a drink from the fountain.

Little did I know but a woman who knew my mother saw me do that and told on me. Mama told me she would take care of it without telling Papa, but if it ever happened again, Papa would know. Much as I loved my Papa and he loved me, I also knew he dispensed the ultimate punishment, and I did not want that. The ultimate punishment for me would be to have him be so very disappointed in me.

1939, The Dance

I was thinking about a time I was about 13 years old. At times there were dances in the school gym, and I wanted to go. Mama said that if I asked Papa, he would say no. I guess I must have begged her a little, and she came up with an idea.

She said I could go, but I had to be home before he got back from work. Papa was an architect in Kiev and worked long hours on government projects. But, of course, that night, Papa came home early.

"Where's Valia?"

I don't know what Mama told him, but he marched himself down to the school gym and walked in. He didn't make a scene when he saw me. He just walked over and took me by the arm and walked me home.

"But, Papa, it was just an innocent dance."

He said, "You are 13 years old. Until you are 18, you are not making your own decisions about this. I am the one deciding, and I am deciding that you are too young." I know he was most upset because he had not been told. Mama and Papa would disagree about some things, but they discussed everything without shouting or even sounding angry.

Our House and My Memories with Papa

Papa and Mama were so sweet together. I just have no memory of seeing them act unkindly to each other. Papa never drank alcohol like lots of Russian men did. When Papa and Mama got married, Mama moved into the communal apartment building that Papa lived in at the top of the hill above the Dnieper River. They lived on the third floor. This large building had once been the luxurious home for one family.

It was a five-story stone building built sometime around 1790. I learned during a later trip to Russia that the entire area on that hill had once been a desired place to live or to visit. During that time, of course, the monarchy reigned, and you were either wealthy or a peasant. It had been taken over by the Communists during the revolution, and when I lived there from about 1926–1941, it had been divided into smaller living units. Residents were Jewish or someone like my Papa who refused to join the Communist party.

The first floor was devoted to shops such as bread, or fabric and threads. The face of the building was flat except where the stairwell went up the center. As I recall, there were at least five floors. Tall windows covered the building about four feet apart. Each window had a keystone top, and each floor was divided horizontally with a dentil frieze. The entrance was level with the sidewalk on the street. You came in through dark, wooden French doors perhaps eight feet tall with four panels of vertical glass above the doors. Inside, the foyer floor was red tiles inlaid in the center of the floor with hexagonal shapes of white marble. Surrounding that was an inlay maze of black-and-white marble. As a child, I loved to play hopscotch on the white marble tiles. I saw that floor on a return trip I made to Russia in the nineties.

Our apartment was on the third floor of this five-story house. Our room was the first door on the left. Papa had gotten that apartment when he was a single man, and now it included Mama and me.

The largest room, which also had a smaller space that looked like a closet, was taken by a Jewish family of six or seven. The mother and father were both medical doctors. A grandmother lived with them, and she was very ill and dying. The other children were younger, like me, except for one older boy/man. He was a violinist for the symphony. Whenever I hear classical violin music now, I want to cry from both the beauty and the sadness of it. I loved hearing him play. That music was like bringing sunshine and hope into our lives.

The third family sharing this space had four people. Their room also had something like a small closet. Each family had a private entrance to their room from the hall. Each of these rooms had a wood burning fireplace in it. The fireplace was very small and made of a white-looking rock built into the corner of the room.

We all shared one toilet, which you also entered from the hall. It was in a small room by itself and was just a toilet. No sink. It flushed by pulling a chain that hung high above the tank.

We all also shared the kitchen which was in a space that had formerly been a luxurious bath. It had a bathtub that no longer worked, so a wooden platform was laid over the top of it, and each family stored their dishes there. Each family also had one burner lit by a kerosene tank. The tank had to be pumped to get it lit. Water was available in this kitchen space we shared. Everyone was respectful. We had to be. Thirteen of us shared one toilet and one small space to cook our meals.

Now, you may start to wonder how we kept clean. During the week, people would get water in a portable basin, take it to their room, and wash off as best they could from that basin. On weekends, people went to the public showers. There were separate shower rooms for men and women. They were completely public. I remember being embarrassed seeing my modest mother in the nude, but over time, I became very accustomed to seeing all kinds of bodies, and I never thought anymore about it. The showerheads were as large as a saucer, unlike the small ones we have here in America today. This type of living condition was just the normal way of life in Stalin's Russia. Everyone lived this way.

In this Communist-controlled, one-room apartment in which we lived, we had a radio with a speaker, like all the other apartments. You could turn it on or off, but you had no ability to control what came through those speakers. We heard only things that the government wanted us to hear. It could be music or propaganda. Many people wanted to hear other things. Papa was one of those people.

I knew that in the corner of our small room hiding under the cover of a piece of cloth were hundreds—even thousands—of pieces of wire and a welding tool. Papa worked with those items and built a radio. We never talked about it. As I think about it now, I believe I just knew never to ask or never talk about it to anyone else.

I only realized after the war that Papa must have wanted to hear what was going on in the rest of the world. But to do so risked death to himself and his family. One night, I heard him whisper to Mama, "Nadia, wake up. Come hear this beautiful music." Papa loved music. I loved music too. I still do, but I just knew, without being told, that this was something secret and possibly dangerous, and I should not even act like I knew anything about it.

Glenda: As soon as Vallie told me about this, she stopped talking and appeared serious. I waited awhile before saying, "You're quiet now. Was there something else?"

I just remembered the music from the violinist and another lady in the building that sang opera. Those were such beautiful sounds. But there was another sound. It was the sound that terrified everyone. My bed was against the wall, and on the other side of that wall was the landing for the stairs. Occasionally, during the night, we would be startled awake by the sound of the main door to the building being thrown open and slammed shut with a loud bang. Then we would hear the sound of boots stomping up those marble stairs. The boots had metal cleats on the bottom of them. I still feel afraid when I see tall, black boots worn with the pants tucked in. I'd hear the boots coming up the stairs. They did not attempt to be quiet. In fact, the louder they were, the more fear they instilled, and that was the plan. If they made it to the third-floor landing outside our door, my heart would beat out of my chest. No one even whispered, but we knew we were all awake. Were they coming for my papa tonight? Did they learn about the radio?

I'd hold my breath and wait for the loud pounding on the door. If they turned the corner and went on up the stairs, I'd release my breath and feel so relieved. But it couldn't all be relief because somewhere in the building, I could hear the banging on a door and sometimes screaming. The next day, another person would be gone.

Glenda: I always associated those boots and terrors with Nazis.

Oh, no, honey. These were Stalin's men. Stalin had created his own reign of terror before the Germans ever came. In fact, by the time the Germans came, many people hoped it would be to rescue us from Stalin's terror, which included deliberate starvation of his people.

Glenda: You look weary. Do you want to take a break?

We both got up. I put my arms around her and held her a minute. Memories like that need a break. We had some tea and chatted about trivial things. Then I asked if she would like to talk about her papa, either now or some other time.

I love talking about Papa. Papa was a very smart man. He got lots of recognition for his work. I have a watch he once received for something he did. Another time, there was to be a celebration for the opening of a building he had worked on that was for officials of the Communist Party. Children were invited to come. I must have been about 10 years old around 1936, and Papa decided I could go with him. Mama did the best she could to get me dressed up suitable for the occasion.

It was so exciting to go to places with Papa. He was handsome, and people admired him. We walked into this magnificent building. Inside were movies, dancing, and puppet shows. Such excitement and fun filled up the place. We had been given a membership to attend other times, but I don't remember it ever happening. I don't know why except Papa did not want to be associated with the Communist Party. It was a time and a world where no one, especially children, asked too many questions.

One day every week, usually on the weekend, Papa would spend

9

the day with me. I suppose it was nice for Mama because it was just the two of us all weeklong as Papa worked long hours designing buildings and overseeing the work. Once I was born, Mama stayed home with me. So Papa and I would go down the hill to the main street of Kiev. I realize now that they sacrificed a lot of time and as much money as they could to make a life for me, their only child, seem as normal and happy as possible. One time, he took me on a horse and buggy ride around the city.

Kiev had a football stadium (Americans would call it soccer). In the winter, the ground was covered with water, and it turned into a large ice rink. People would come and rent skates. I was pretty good at skating because I had my own skates, and I played on frozen patches of ice lots of times. Papa was not so good.

One day, we both got on skates, and I, being a little smarty, took off without him. I'd look back for him, but he was so slow. Kids would hold up this little flag in their hands while they skated. It was a treat to have one. It was a red Communist flag, but we didn't care what it meant. We just loved to ice-skate and hold this little flag and to hear the noise it made as the breeze blew through it while we moved around.

There weren't restaurants everywhere like we have in Portland today, but you could buy ice cream from a street vendor. Yes, ice cream, even in that cold weather. It was such a treat. Since there was no place to sit, we would stand at these tall tables like a pole with a circle top on it. You see them now in airport fast-food areas some-times. Papa would always get ice cream for me but never for himself.

One summer when I was around 8 years old, I remember noticing that grown-up men and women would walk together with the woman holding onto her companion's arm which was bent at the elbow. I wanted to walk with my papa like that. I was getting taller and hoped I could soon be able to reach his arm, but he was at least six feet tall, and I so short that I would try to reach his bent arm, but it just didn't work. He would chuckle and smile at me.

No florist shops existed as we have here today. In the summer, people stood on the street and sold flowers from a basket. I loved roses, but there were no roses. Yet, in my active imagination, I had this idea that I was so small that I could climb onto a rose petal and float.

On one exceptional day when we were out walking, we saw some roses in a window. Papa bought one for me, and I cannot tell you how special I felt walking around with him holding my hand and me holding that beautiful, long stem rose. I dried that rose and saved it for years.

I often asked Mama and Papa to tell me a particular story over and over. I loved it. They told me that one day they were out walking together and saw some beautiful and very large cabbages. They touched the leaf of one and then heard a voice coming from inside the cabbage. "Michael," Mama said, "let's pull this cabbage up and take it home." He said they couldn't take it because he thought it was someone else's cabbage. As a child when I heard this story, I would think, "That's me, and they're going to leave me here." But Papa agreed, and they took the cabbage home. Once home, they began to pull off the leaves of the cabbage, and in the center . . . was ME sitting there on a tiny rose petal.

When the time came that we were separated, I think hope helped me too. I hoped and I believed that someday, I was going to tell my Papa what happened, and he would take care of it. And I would so often think, "No one will ever believe what is happening to the other people and to me. Except for Papa. Papa will believe me." And later, especially in the camp, I kept holding onto that belief . . . even though I knew that Papa was dead.

Grandparents

Papa's parents lived in the farmlands of Ukraine. We had to get there by train, so we didn't go very often. The country had so many fields, and the food for most of Ukraine came from those farms. When Communism came, they took over the farms and organized them into co-op farms. Farmers were allowed one cow. My grandparents' cow was named Marucia. She lived in the house. Well, not in the house. Let me draw you a picture. It was all under the same roof but not in the same room. It was the way everyone lived in the country. Grandpa built the house himself, using wood for the tall ceilings, and it had a straw roof. Sometimes I would help him gather straw to add to the roof.

Imagine a square room with a door entering from the outside. When you stepped over the threshold and through that door, you were in Marucia's room. The floor was dirt with straw. As you stood there facing the back wall, that was her feeding trough. To your right was another door. You would take one step up through that door, which took you into the main house.

So imagine a slightly larger room in the shape of a rectangle. There was a wooden table with benches on each side. Grandpa built the cooking stove. It was a stone fireplace where they burned wood for cooking and heating. The other side of that fireplace then became the head of the bed. The bed was short and not too wide, but it was the bed for both of my grandparents. When I stayed with them, I remember each of them lay on their side facing each other with their knees curled up to fit on the bed, and I lay between them. Light came through one small window which had glass in it.

The village had one well which was just outside their house. It was the kind of well that has a round stone wall and a wooden bucket which hung from a beam across the top. The bucket was on a rope. We would let the rope go down into the well. It was attached to a crank with a handle that we would turn to bring the water back up. Then we'd pour the water into our own bucket.

Grandpa was more physical, emotional, and playful than Grandma. He would pick me up and toss me into the air and catch me and laugh.

Grandma nourished us with her cooking. She was serious and stern. One time, Grandma was upset with me. I was maybe 5, 6, or 7. The kids had made up a story about a wedding. They had made me the bride. They put white paper or a rag over my head. Grandma came out and saw this and jerked that veil off my head and said, "This is no game for children." Grandma seemed always to be working. I can picture her hanging out clothes to dry and beating rugs with a rug beater. She showed love with all her work. But Grandpa could hug and kiss and play also.

The country children loved to hear my stories of the city. They had never seen buildings taller than one story, so when they learned I lived in a tall building, and we lived on the third floor, they wanted to hear all about it.

Mma's parents were city people. When I was born in Kiev, her father was already dead. Her father had owned an ink factory. They lived in a beautiful, private house. He was shot and killed by Stalin's armies around 1918 when the army took power and took over all businesses. All personal wealth was taken away. Grandma ended up living in a shack in a Jewish community along with other formerly prosperous business owners.

Mama had one sister named Manea (Maria), and her son was Victor. She also had a brother Gryscha (George). They all lived together. Grandma was a very religious woman but had also lost the freedom to worship openly. Manea and Gryscha worked so Grandma was the person who took care of Victor. I'll tell you later about the last time I saw my grandmother. It was a very sad and frightening time.

School

My parents were strong believers in education. Even though my father had been raised in the country on a farm, he left the farm for the University of Kiev and received a degree as both an architect and engineer. My mother, Nadia, was raised in the city with her sister, Manea, and brother, Gryscha. I was told later that she and her siblings were educated privately. Besides reading, writing, and mastering arithmetic, Mama was taught to crochet, knit, sew, and cook. She sewed without patterns and learned to cook with whatever she was able to get. These were things it seemed women needed to learn. I really don't know any more about her education.

You see, in those days, people did not talk about themselves or the past. It was just too scary. You didn't know who was listening and why they would want to know. Neighbors turned in neighbors, and family might even report family in order to protect themselves or get some advantage. It was a society where no one could trust anyone else. Remember that the Communists had taken Mama's papa's business and their home, and then they killed her papa.

I know that my parents wanted me to be educated. When I was only 3 years old, my parents took me to this German lady's house. She was weird to me. She wore a dark dress that went down to the ground, and then she wore an all-black, modern-looking hat. She carried a white umbrella. Even at age 3, 4, and 5, I remember how strangely I thought she dressed. She would only accept children that could go to the bathroom by themselves. I remember feeling proud because I could take care of myself that way. She had five or six small children she kept for a few hours. I guess it would be like nursery school. A private nursery school.

The main reason my parents sent me there was to learn German. She would only talk to us in German. We would go to the park, the garden, sing songs, and everything was in German. After I started at the Communist school around age 6, I still went to see her for German lessons.

When I started my first day of first grade, the teacher wanted to see just how much each child knew. Mama had already taught me to read and to write. So this teacher had the letters CAMEL upon the board (it was in Russian, of course) and asked me if I could read the letters and I said the word: camel.

When I was in the fourth grade at my school, we began to study a foreign language. It was German. I was already better than the teacher at that point, so she just had me help grade papers and help her in class.

I didn't like studying another language. I remember asking Papa,

"Why do I have to do this? I will never use it!" I don't remember what he said but look at me now. I am here talking to you today because knowing that language saved my life.

Hospitalized

When I was a child, my tonsils were removed without any anesthetic. Can you believe that? And it was just a day surgery. I went home on the streetcar afterward with Mama. I remember that even though I was a little girl, an older woman stood up and gave me her seat.

When I was about 10 years old, I was in the hospital again, this time to have my appendix removed. Parents were not allowed in the hospital. This nurse took me in and made me undress. I walked into surgery naked! Can you believe that? I was so embarrassed and scared. There were three or four doctors or nurses at the table. I walked up to the table. I guess they helped me get on it. I was just so scared and embarrassed. They put a screen in front of me. There was no anesthetic. They held me down and cut me open. I screamed and screamed. I could feel *everything*. How could they do that? How could they even work hearing someone screaming that way? I learned later that general anesthetic was used only for serious surgeries. Obviously, an appendectomy wasn't considered serious enough. They didn't use sutures either. They just put in these clamps. That time I was in the hospital for 2 weeks healing up before I could go home.

Later, I was in the hospital for 42 days in isolation because I had scarlet fever. Neither Mama nor Papa could come into the hospital, but they would come to the hospital and stand outside. They came every day. I would look out the window to see them. Mama told me that for every day that I didn't cry she would get me a chocolate bar. Do you know how hard it would be to buy that much chocolate? I cried everyday anyway, but when I came home, I had 42 chocolate bars. That and in so many other ways my parents showed me how much they loved me.

Papa Leaves

Sunday, June 22, 1941, announcements came over the speakers in all the apartments that Nazi Germany had invaded the Soviet Union. Papa and I had planned a Sunday walk, but all plans were changing. Schools ended, offices closed, everything was unknown to me but the fear I felt and could see in Mama and Papa.

Everything was changing rapidly. Very shortly after that, perhaps even the next day, Papa was ordered to report for service in the Red Army. Mama started crying. Mama and Papa had already lived through the end of the monarchy, followed by revolutions, civil wars, and World War I. Had they ever known a time of peace and stability in their lives? Maybe they hadn't. And now, Papa was ordered to leave.

My birthday is July 8th. Papa was ordered to report to duty very near my birthday. He got permission to delay his departure so we could celebrate. Not a long delay. Troops were leaving every day. So maybe he easily got permission to leave the next day.

Papa put on his dress shirt and started to put on his tie. I had learned to tie those tricky loops of under, over, up, down, and through, so I stood on a little stool to reach him and tied his necktie while he looked me in the eyes and smiled.

We stepped out of our apartment and walked down the three flights of stairs onto the street. We had gone out together many times in my life, but we knew this day was different. This day was not the lighthearted and fun day we usually had. Papa was quiet and serious. He knew he was leaving, and he had things to say on this day. "Valia, you are going to grow up fast. You will need to take care of Mama." He spoke the truth of what we both knew but had never talked about. He said, "Mama is not a well person. She will need you to take care of her. Stay with her, Valia. Don't let her out of your sight. When this war is over, come back here. I will find you both."

There was little time just to enjoy each other that beautiful day. From a distance, we heard loud and unfamiliar noises getting closer and closer. They were heavy sounds moving slowly. "Run down the hill," Papa yelled at me. We ran and ran down the hill; then Papa yelled at me to drop. I fell to the ground, and my father covered me with his body. We could hear the bombs falling. They missed us as they turned left toward the Dnieper River. The sound got faint; then they turned and came back. The sound was lighter. Later in the war, I had learned they flew faster with an empty load. We got up and ran toward the apartment to get Mama.

The next day, Papa had to leave. He told me, "Valia, remember this. Never leave your mama. Stay together. After the war, I will find you." And he was gone. Mama was screaming, and I was crying. Just before he walked away, I had been standing up against the building outside. I had one leg bent with my foot resting on the building, and I said, "Papa, Papa, I will never see you again."

"Don't say that. Don't say that, Valia."

Then he was gone. It wasn't like me to talk that way to him. Why? Why did I say that? It wasn't like me to talk to him like that. But it turned out to be true.

After Papa had been taken, I came home from school one day and caught Mama sewing pictures into the lining of our coats. We each had one coat. "Mama, what are you doing?"

"I'm sewing these pictures into our coats."

"But why?"

"Just in case we ever get separated."

"But, Mama, we won't. We won't. I told Papa we'd stay together. Always."

One day the following winter, the winter of 1941, an order came that we were to be evacuated immediately. "Take only what you can carry on your body." We wore a dress, our only coat, and somehow, Mama managed to take her fox fur.

We were moved into a small, one-story house in an industrial area. It had two rooms and one toilet. Not with a shower or tub or sink. Just the toilet. The kind with a tank on the top, and you pulled the cord to flush it. We shared the house with another family. You'd walk into the house, and on the right was a door.

A woman lived there with three children under the age of 14. We had to cross through their room and out the door to go into our room, which was very small. But I remember it well. There was one small bed pushed up against the wall. On the right was a window about four by four feet. It had a very wide window ledge that came into the room, and we used it for our table. There was a full-view mirror on the other wall. That mirror seemed such a luxury.

There was no place to have a fire. It was winter and cold, even for Russian.

(The winter of 1941 was reported to be the worst winter in Russia in 100 years.)

There was no money. Any money we had no longer had any value. Food was not available without begging or trading. I remember one day seeing my beautiful, elegant mother walking outside, bent completely over from carrying a load of sticks on her back. It is such a sad memory. I remember thinking, "What can we do with that wood? We don't have a match or any place to have a fire."

It was such a severe time of cold and starvation, and Mama was getting sicker and physically weaker every day. She was doing whatever she could to take care of us. She must have traded those sticks for food. I remember a day we traded a button from my coat for a rotten potato.

Maria

I feel like we talk about too many sad things, and you might think that nothing good ever happened. You know, so many people helped to save my life. And Mama's. Last night, I thought about Maria. She was an angel. Why had I not already told you about her? I cried I felt so guilty that I had not yet told you about Maria.

Glenda: Many of your stories have been of wonderful people, or they have been funny stories. Do you want to tell me about Maria now? Were you still in Kiev?

Yes. This was in Kiev. It was after Papa had been taken. Mama and I were living in this one room in an apartment in a bombed building. Everyone was starving. Mama was so sick. She had boils on her legs. We couldn't even get a little hot water to clean her sores. There was no food.

I decided to venture out to see if I could find something. It was cold. Everything was snow covered. The only way to get anywhere was to walk, and we would walk long distances, but we were used to it. Papa had been the supervisor on many of the buildings in Kiev, and I walked to one he had helped to build. I had been in and around that building many times. I knew the ins and outs of it. Gates surrounded all of the buildings, but I knew where the back gate of this building was and how to get in.

I was feeling desperately scared, hungry, and missing Papa. I walked past a door, and it suddenly opened. A man in a white hat and white apron emptied a big bowl of potato peelings. I was carrying a metal pot that was shaped with a bend in it so that it fit around your side and sat on your hip. It had a handle. I've never seen pots like that here, but they were common then in Russia. I began to fill that pot with those potato peelings. I pushed and pushed and stuffed all the peelings I could get into that pot.

Suddenly, the door opened again, and there stood this beautiful lady in a white nurse's uniform. She spoke to me in German. "Mädchen, mädchen," meaning girl, girl, "What are you doing here?" I answered her in German.

"Oh, you speak German, do you?"

"Yes."

"Why are you here?"

"My mother is ill, and we have no food. We are starving."

"Just a minute. You stay here. I'll be back."

She left and came back with a small package wrapped in brown paper. "You take this to your mother. The next time you come back, knock on the door, and the man will let me know you are here. Good-bye." She put her arm on my shoulder. That touch of kindness felt so good.

I opened the gate and went out onto the street where I opened the package, and I found some bread. Do you know how long it had been since we had bread? And what else I keep remembering in these stories is there are so few people outside.

Where are the people? Are they lost in my memory? Did I always just feel so alone? Where are the people? I know that many, many had died already of starvation. Most of the men had been taken. Many Jews and others had been taken away also. Maybe others were too sick and too scared to go outside.

I took the package home, and that night, we had bread and potato peels. I remember they were cooked a little bit. But how did we do that? We had no electricity, no wood. We had no way to start a fire. But let's say someone found a match and got a fire started. Others would get a little fire from it. We probably shared those potato peelings with someone who helped us get a fire. I don't remember.

With all those people dying from starvation, where were they buried? Who dug the graves? It was winter. The ground was frozen.

(I later learned through research that bodies tended to be stored in basements of large buildings. They remained frozen until they could be buried.)

I went back to the building other times. I don't remember how many. Maria gave me two addresses. One was her personal address, and the other was the address of her mother who I think lived in Czechoslovakia. She always gave me a piece of bread. But soon I too was gone.

I've often wondered why I never hated Germans. I just never could, honey. A German gave me bread when I was hungry. They also captured me, but another German saved me when I was in prison.

There were others during this harsh winter of German occupation when I was 16 years old. Again, as always, I was so hungry, and Mama so ill. Some of the German soldiers were on top of a building. They would lower a rope down from the side of the building. I would tie my little pot on the rope, and they would pull it up and put a little food in it. I would untie it and run home as fast as I could to give it to

Mama. See, some had a heart. Not all of them were bad. Maybe they didn't even know what Hitler was doing. Maybe they couldn't believe what Stalin was doing when they got there and saw the deliberate destruction of his own people by starvation.

My thoughts: And maybe they were learning how easy it would be to tempt people to come to them when they were ready to load up trucks and trains.

I guess I am ready to tell you about my friend, Lida. We were best friends. It was hard to have friends. People were growing up in such distrust of each other. People were disappearing all the time. People starved, were sick, and scared. But Lida and I played with each other. She helped make life have some joy. Her father had been a watch-maker. Well, while Mama and I were in this apartment, a printed order was distributed ordering all Jewish people to report . . . Oh, honey . . . I don't know if I can tell this . . . report to the cemetery. They had to report the next morning. All our people . . . all our friends were Jewish. The order said to bring only jewelry.

You know, some people had disabled people and old people in their family, so that night, they were working hard to make carts or something they could pull these people on. The next morning, a river of people flowed past the window—all moving in the same direction. Mama didn't want me to look. But I had to look—all those people moving in the same direction, and the sound of feel shuffling in the dirt. Once in a while, you could hear a little *kuthump, kuthump* from a wooden wheel turning as it pulled the sick and elderly.

But you know what I remember so much to this day? It was so quiet. So quiet. No one was talking. No one was crying. Not even the babies were crying. And then little Lida looked up and saw me. She started jumping and pointing to her watch and motioned for me to come get it. Mama wouldn't let me. That's the last time I saw Lida.

What they did . . . I don't know if I can tell this.

They marched those people up to the top of the hill to this cem-etery and ordered the men to dig a grave—a big pit, narrow but very long. Mama and I did not watch but those who did told us later what happened. They lined the women and children up on one side and then started shooting. The fathers and husbands watched. Can you even imagine this? Can you believe what I am telling you? And you know, not everyone died. You could hear babies cry and people scream. And so there was more shooting. Then they lined the men up and started the shooting again. The last men left had to sprinkle bags of lime over the bodies to help them decompose and then cover the graves with dirt. When the job was done, they lined the last men up on the edge of the cliff and shot them. They fell into the Dnieper River.

We learned about it as it happened. There had been people at the foot of the cliff watching. They saw the bodies falling and the blood flowing in the river. We lived at that time only two or three blocks from this cliff and the edge of the river. Some had asked us to go watch, but we couldn't. We didn't.

Papa in the War

The next part of this story I learned about 55 years later when I found the woman that Papa had married after Mama died. She told me all that she knew based only on what Papa was willing to tell her.

The government had sent him papers saying they would protect him if he would help to rebuild the country after the war was over. He reported for duty. They assigned him a high rank that put him in charge of 1,000 soldiers. They were only boys. Children. Sixteen and 17 years old. Their assignment was to go wherever they were told to protect the country against the Germans. Supplies were short. They weren't even given proper clothing. They had little to nothing to protect themselves. The government told them they would have to use their numbers for protection, and when the Germans saw there were so many of them, they would be too scared to attack. My father knew that would not be true. They would all be killed if they tried to fight. He knew they could not protect themselves without weapons. When they got to their destination, Papa decided he would tell his men.

As a group, the men decided to surrender. The Germans took all of them prisoners. The Germans herded them onto trains going through Kiev on their way to Poltava Prison. It was winter, and there was always deep, blowing snow.

Now how my dad did this next thing, I will never know. I'll just call it all a miracle. He found or he had a small piece of white paper. On it, he wrote his name and the address where we were living when he was taken. Somehow, he managed to slip that piece of paper through the train, and it flew out. White paper onto white snow in a town of millions of people.

A woman picked that paper up and walked with it to the address. When she saw the Germans now occupied the building, she must have found someone who told her we had been forced to move and gave her some directions or address. She walked farther to find the room Mama and I were now living in. Oh, Mama was so happy. She kept hugging this stranger and thanking her. She wanted to give her something for all the effort she made, but, honey, we didn't even have a crust of bread to share with her. That is one of my saddest memories. Mama was such a gracious lady. We wanted to give her something other than our thanks and relief to know that Papa was still alive.

Poltava Prison

Everyone knew about Poltava Prison. Hundreds of prisoners died there every day. Prisoners were packed behind fences with no place to get indoors from the cold and were not given enough food to live.

A group of women in the area had learned that if you went to Poltava, there was a book listing the names of prisoners. You could learn if your loved one was there alive or had died. Some of Mama's friends came to the house. "Nadia, we are going. We want you to go with us." Mama was too sick to go. She would never be able to walk that far.

"Please, Mama, I want to go."

I thought maybe—maybe—I could see my papa just one more time. These friends of ours promised Mama they would take care of me like I was their own child.

Now, I have to go back and tell you another story, so you will understand what happened next.

Before the war, Mama dressed in nice clothes. She made them herself, and she did a wonderful job. There was a fashion of wearing fox fur—the whole fox around your neck. Can you just see it? It was the whole fox with its head and the mouth hanging open on one side of you, and hanging down the other side was the fox tail. Now, we did not have much money, but somehow, Papa had managed one day before the war to come home with a beautiful box. Inside for Mama was not only a fox fur but the more desirable silver fox fur. It was the most beautiful thing I had ever seen. She said we could share it when I got older. There was a long mirror in the room we had, so I would put that fur around me and look at myself, and my imagination would go wild. I loved it.

When I got ready to leave with these women to go to Poltava to try to find Papa, Mama said I had to take this fur and use it to get something to eat. "Please, Mama, do we have to?" She said it was the only thing we had left. For that fur, I got one stale loaf of bread and two big chunks of bacon. Not sliced bacon like we are used to buying in stores today but big chunks. I thought I could keep one, and I'd give one to Papa.

Walking was not easy. The ground was covered with snow. There were no roads. There were mines, and the Germans occupied all the area. We had very little food. I remember we walked for at least 2 days, sleeping at night in places such as a barn. I only remember sleeping on straw. It was country. Farmers had fields and barns. Farmers were better off during this time. If they had even a potato, they could bring it to the city and swap it. There was no money then. Money was worthless. Everything was traded.

Finally, from a far distance, we could see a fence that seemed to stretch as far as you could see. People seemed to be in a line along that fence like they were looking and waiting for something. What I saw as we got closer was they were digging graves in that frozen ground to bury the hundreds or more of people who were dying every day. No one was dressed for the bitter cold.

(Vallie began weeping now, remembering this.)

We found the building and got into the line. German soldiers were shouting things like, "Not here. Move on. Get away. Move it." They were pushing and shoving. I was so scared.

When my turn came, I was shaking inside, and I told the German my papa's name: Michael Kopytina.

He looked in his book and abruptly said, "He's dead. Move on."

"Why?" I asked. He told me something I couldn't understand, and I remember nothing else. I don't even remember anything about coming back home.

I lived until 1990 believing my papa died there. But all that time, he was alive.

By the summer of 1942, Mama was feeling a little better. I was about to turn 16 years old. Someone told us that there was a man who knew Papa in prison. We had to go see this man. I ask Mama, "Where is this man?" Mama answered that he was at his home.

I'll never forget walking by a short brick building that had a flower box on the outside that was filled with beautiful, colorful flowers in full bloom, and Mama was saying, "Hurry up. You have always been distracted by beautiful flowers."

"Yes. You know it."

Well, the next thing I remember, we were in a room in this man's house. Mama was sitting on a small chair facing this man who was also sitting in a chair with nothing between them. I was standing behind Mama. He told her that there were six or seven who planned an escape from Poltava. Papa was a big help in making the plans, but when the time came to leave, he wouldn't go. He said, "I had a thousand young men in my charge. I can't leave them here."

Mama was so upset. "How could he do that? How could he do that?" I remember thinking, "That's my papa. Why can't you understand that?"

By winter, German trucks were in the streets all the time. They were everywhere. Everyone was hungry all the time. Our main goal was survival: we had to eat and stay together. Mama was sick. She continued to have boils all over her legs and thighs. I think she had a fever. She coughed a lot. Looking back, I would say she was also severely depressed because she had lost her ability to make decisions for us and be in charge. It got to the point where I was beginning to feel like I needed to take care of her instead of my Mama taking care of me. Most of the men were all gone already. No one was left but women and children and a few old men.

On this particular day, we needed to go see Mama's mama. Mama's father was killed when Stalin took over. He had been a wealthy man who owned an ink factory. When they killed him, they took his business, big house, and everything he owned. His wife, Manea (Maria), and their son, Victor, lived with Grandma along with my mother's brother, Gryscha (George). I'll never forget the day I last saw all of them. My grandma was dying. We wanted to see her one more time because things were happening fast. People were disappearing.

We walked to a place that I remember as looking like a barn. That doesn't make sense to me because this was in the city of Kiev, and there were no barns. Anyway, we went inside, and the floor of this room was just straw. Grandma lay there on a blanket on the straw with nothing but an old, dirty rag covering her. Victor, now 16 years old, was kneeling by her head. Grandma had been the main person that raised Victor, and he loved her very much. Cloth covered Grandma's face. I was holding onto Mama's left hand. Victor started to lift the cloth from Grandma's face, and Mama embraced my face to her chest and would not let me look. It seemed to be urgent that we leave, but Victor would not go. I never learned what happened to him.

The next thing that happened couldn't have been more than 2 weeks later. We were wandering the streets looking for food. German trucks were driving around in the streets, but on this day, we noticed something different. People were gathering around the trucks. I mean, it looked like they were going voluntarily and not forced. So we joined them, hoping for some handout to eat. German soldiers had given away food before. Maybe they were now.

When we got to the trucks, people were loaded into the back, and a guard yelled at Mama and me to get into the truck too. Some people were crying, and others said at least now we would be able to eat. They packed us into the back of the truck like sardines. This was a big military truck with a canopy over the top and sides.

They took us to a train and began to force us into it. It was some kind of a storage car. One of those long cars that have two big metal doors that slide together, and then on the outside of the door, a big bar drops down. Nothing inside could get out. At the train, there were soldiers with guns everywhere. They pushed and pushed to get as many people as they could into the train. There was not even room to sit. There was no food and no room to go to the bathroom. Some people, like Mama, were sick. If you had to go to the bathroom . . . Well, you just had to do it standing up right there where you were. Can you imagine? All these people who lived clean lives respecting privacy to be in such a situation?

The train traveled all night, and that first night they stopped the train, and the doors opened. Mama was coughing as were others. Some instinct made me realize they were going to get rid of some of the people. They began sorting us, and I started whispering, "Mama, Mama." She was moaning from pain. A guard grabbed hold of her and started pulling. I hung on her with Papa's voice in my head, "Never let go. Hold Mama's hand, and I will find you. Don't let go." It was over so fast. The guard pulled her from my hand and threw her off the train. She dropped into the deep, deep snow. With one firm hand, the guard pushed me back into the train, shut the door, then the bar crashed down.

That's the last time I ever saw my mama. She was lying in this deep snow. The train started again, and we left.

That has been one of my saddest lingering memories all these years. I never found her or Papa after the war, but many years later, I learned they both got back to Kiev, but I didn't. They never knew what happened to me. I'm sure they assumed I was dead because if I were alive, I'd come back to Kiev and find them.

I later came to understand that there were good people all over Europe trying to rescue and save others. I think she got rescued. She had to have been rescued. If Nazis were left with those old and sick people, they would just kill them. But instead of killing them, it seems they left them there in the snow to die. Many years later when I met my stepmother, she said that Papa wouldn't talk about it.

CHAPTER 2

Auschwitz, 1942

The Arrival

THE NEXT TIME the train stopped, we were in Warsaw, Poland, at a camp called Auschwitz. The doors of the train opened, and eight to 10 German officers were looking over the arrivals. They unloaded us and marched us to barracks where all but our dresses were taken.

There was such a commotion. Lots of people were speaking Russian and German. I could understand both, and I could hear a German asking, "Can anyone here speak German?" I didn't volunteer. I was so confused, scared, lost, and feeling hopeless and alone.

Women in line were all talking about "getting burned." They were using fire and burning numbers on our bodies. We were in this line, and I was so afraid of getting burned too. An SS woman was walking down the line shouting orders. When she came to me, I said, "I am not even Jewish. Why am I here?" She just kept walking past me but said, "Well, get out of line."

I was just thinking, "Where's Mama? Where's Papa?" It was all I wanted to know, but I knew Papa was dead. Mama had been thrown off the train into the snow because she was so sick. She probably died overnight.

But I was still in a line (the same one? I don't know), and when it came to my turn, I spoke to them in German, and this soldier pulled me out and sent me to another room. He left me there, and I was alone. He soon came back into the room, and I was crying. He asked me questions about my father and my mother. Where were they born? Where are you from? Who were your grandparents? He said he had to send me with the rest of the people.

"But why am I being punished? I never did anything wrong. I never broke the law." He just said that I had to go to the camp. "I think a mistake has been made," he said. "Maybe I can help you later, but no one can help at this point."

I remember him so clearly. He had on a sharply pressed uniform. It was so clean. I remember it had no wrinkles, and his left arm was missing. Totally gone because the left sleeve of his uniform jacket laid flat all the way up to his shoulder, and it came down and was tucked neatly into his pants. I told him that I had lost my parents. I don't remember all the things we talked about, but he said that he would try to get me out of this.

(It is at this point where it may be understood why Vallie never was tattooed. History of Auschwitz shows that thousands of non-Jews, and especially Russians, were pulled out of the lines, not tattooed, and put into "service" for Germany. Most were the men who were sent out as laborers and literally worked to death. The Germans saw another job for this young, attractive, blond, blue-eyed girl. She and others who were chosen for the same work were put in holding areas together.)

The Cell

This memory has been the source of one of my worst nightmares. I don't know how or exactly when or why this happened. They took me out and put me into a hole. A hole? A cell? It was dark. A desk stood on the left. I could barely make out a woman sitting at the desk. There were no windows, and it was very dark, but I could see her, but barely. Somebody came and took me by the hand or elbow, and a door opened. There were two doors. One was a solid door, and the other one had pretty scrollwork on it.

I was pushed through these doors, which then closed behind me. I was left alone. It was total darkness now. It stank. I could not see anything, and I was so scared. I found a wall and put my right hand on it and started slowly walking along the wall. The wall was wet and cold. I touched straw with my feet. I reached down and felt around it. Maybe it was intended to sleep on, but I never did. I kept moving and bumped into a table and a bench.

I don't remember crying then like I do now when I remember this cell.

I had to go to the bathroom. I walked on and touched a bucket that was overflowing with urine. I got all wet with urine when I bumped into it.

Outside the door, I heard women screaming so loud. Screaming, "No. Don't. Please don't." Different voices of women screaming. That terrified me so. It sounded like they were being tortured. I couldn't imagine how. I was so scared. I didn't cry. I guess I was just too scared to cry.

At some point, I heard steps coming to my door. I was so afraid someone was coming to torture me.

The steps stopped outside my door, and a little door at the bottom opened briefly. A dish was pushed through. It was food, but I couldn't eat. I don't remember eating anything.

I don't know how long they left me in that cell. I don't know why I was there. I know when they came to get me, I still had my clothes on from when I was first picked up, and my hair was still long.

Clothes

Next thing I remember, and I don't even know if it goes with this time, but it seems it must be close, I was with other women, but no one talked. We were around a large, steaming kettle. Someone told us to take off all our clothes and put them in the kettle. The embarrassment was beyond description. No one was used to being public with nudity. In my home, I never even saw my parents in their underwear. In the public showers we went to, I tried not to look at the other women and children. Then someone just dumped a pile of clothes out and told us to find something to wear. People were searching to find something that fit but soon settled on anything to just be covered.

They put us into cells with a large group of other women. One night, a woman guard opened the door and started pointing. "You, you, you. Come with me." She chose about six girls, and I was one of them. She gave us army coats to put around us; then we climbed onto the back of a truck. I was about 16 years old. We didn't talk to one another. I didn't know what was happening, but the others seemed happy. We had been told we could get food. That made me happy. But I was scared too.

The truck stopped. It was dark. When we got off, we found a group of officers waiting, maybe eight or so, and they seemed happy. I remember happy because it had been so long since I had seen anyone happy.

The men chose us one by one. One came and put his arm around me and said, "Come with me."

We were out in this field, and there were small rooms. Well, more like a little building but just the size of one very small room. It looked like a playhouse with one window off to the side and one door right in the middle. He took me inside, where there was a table and a chair on one side. There was a twin-size bed, and on the bed was a pillow and a folded blanket. The room was square with the bed coming toward the middle of the room from the corner.

It just seemed strange in such a small area to use up that much space with that arrangement. The details I remember sometimes are also strange to me.

(There was a prolonged pause).

Glenda: And then what happened?

Well, I was so scared, and I was crying. He said, "Come here," so I went to him. He asked me, "Have you ever been with a man before?"

"No. Never." I was still crying and so scared. This man was old enough to be my father. Maybe even older than my father. He said, "Promise me you will never ever tell anyone, and I will promise you I won't touch you. Just go lie down and go to sleep."

I said, "I can't sleep. I'm too scared." He told me to bring the blanket to him, which I did, and he wrapped it around me like a mummy, then he lifted me and lay me on the bed and then lay down beside me.

The next morning I woke up and saw him sitting on the chair at the table with his head down on his folded hands. I also saw that a stove was in the corner. I hadn't noticed it the night before. I guess I was too scared and sleepy.

That is a sweet memory for me from all those years. I've often wondered if he had a daughter about my age, and he just couldn't take advantage of me.

That wasn't the last time I was taken out and used for sex. But I have to say that I don't ever remember anyone being violent with me.

There were other officers, but I don't remember any pleasure or pain ever. This may sound crazy, but it was like I wasn't there. It was like I floated out and got to a corner of the room and just waited until it was over. Does that mean I'm crazy? I never wanted anyone to know that.

Glenda: No, you are not, nor were you, crazy. There is a word we use for that—disassociation. It is a wonderful way our mind and spirit can protect us from truly awful things. Isn't it great you can't remember? I have heard from many people who have been abused about "leaving their body and watching," or they just don't remember. But you said you did remember something else.

It was probably a different time, but I remember waking up in a room with a window and a shade on it. If you were standing in the doorway, on the right was a small bed with a little table beside it. On the left wall was something like tile. There was a stove in the corner. It seems like there was a hole in the wall and something like a pipe that seemed to go into the outside wall. Anyway, here is what I remember. I was on that bed against the wall, and I saw the back of this man. He was fully dressed in a uniform and had a hat on. He was stuffing a bloody rag into that opening in that stove pipe or whatever it was. That's all I remember.

I also knew the blood was not from having a period. That had actually started when I was about 14 years old and living in Ukraine, but it didn't last long. I assumed years later it was because of all the starvation in Ukraine. No one was healthy.

Camp Conditions

One day when they came to get us as usual, they took me away and shaved off all my hair. Using me for sex was over. We had never been fed well, and I guess they just used us as long as we looked OK. When we started getting emaciated and covered in lice, our job was over, and newer, healthier girls were taken. I would say it probably lasted 8 or 9 months.

After that, some got chosen to get outside the cell for other jobs. Those who had to stay in saw it as a privilege to get out. So for a while, I had my second job which was riding the train to Dacha to the other concentration camps. People were being delivered there, and my job was to sort the clothes and the shoes. If I found any jewelry, I was to turn it in. I never remember finding any. Everything had been taken from the prisoners by this time.

At this time I was living, if you can call it that, with about 60 women. We were kept in a cell about ten feet by twenty. There was one small window near the top. We were allowed outside our cell briefly during the day to get light and air. Guards and German shepherds surrounded us. Those dogs controlled the area, and if we got even an inch outside the allowed space, they would bite.

I never got bitten.

During these days, I cried a lot, and the guards hated it. Once we were standing in a lineup, and an officer yelled at me to stop crying. "Stop or else," he screamed. Then he reached for his *knuple* (whip) and slung it at me. I reached up my hand to protect my face. It hit my hand and cut it open.

I still have the scar right here next to my thumb.

My body—everyone's body—was nothing but skin stretched over bones. The thin dress over me no longer fit. My hair was gone except for about a quarter of an inch. I don't know why I remember that. Maybe it was the only thing about my body I could remember that seemed a little familiar, the only thing they could not permanently take away from me—my hair.

This room or cell we were in was so small for 60 people that we had to stand. To sleep, we had to line up, then lie on our side. There was no room to lie on our backs or to roll over. And every morning, some would be dead.

I think it was then that Rosa the Gypsy was so dear to me. She took care of me like a mother. She held on to me during the nights. One day, she had a little tiny piece of dry bread to eat. Where it came from, I don't know. She was dying. Starving to death. I feel ashamed to tell you what happened next. That night, I ate that tiny piece of her bread. The next morning she was dead.

I can't tell you the extremes people will go to, to survive. Some people drank urine. A rumor was going around that it could help you live. When we were outside, we risked being attacked by the dogs by getting up close to the fence and looking for a blade of grass. Just a single blade of grass to eat.

These things are very hard for me to remember. I haven't talked about most of them to anyone.

Do you want to know what we had to eat then? In the mornings, we were given a cup of hot water and a little chunk of bread. The bread actually had sawdust in it. Sometimes you would get a splinter in your mouth from eating that bread. In the afternoon, two women would carry in a big metal pot. It had handles on each side. They would set the kettle down, and all of us in the room would get our cup filled. It had some flavor to it, but I can tell you there was never anything of solid substance in it. Oh, how we talked about our dream of finding a potato peeling or something to add to that stuff they called "soup."

One day, a girl about 14 years old was taken out to go work in the kitchen to pull feathers off chickens. Women talked about how lucky she was. When she came back that day, she had sneaked back a small piece of chicken fat. Women were rushing and pushing to look at it and get a lick of it. Suddenly, a female guard burst into the room and pulled the girl out and beat her up. She beat her so badly that they brought her back into the cell on a stretcher and dropped it down on the floor.

This is so hard, so hard to remember . . .

She died. How can there be such cruelty? How? They wanted to teach us what would happen if we didn't obey or tried to take any advantage of a situation.

The Shower

One day, we were surprised to be told we were going to get a shower. We had to take off our dirty dresses, and then we were all marched into this shower room. We were packed in there holding our breasts trying to cover ourselves up. In spite of everything, we still were modest. There may have been a hundred of us. The room was a large concrete space with showers overhead.

But something must have gone wrong. The showers weren't working. I was on the side near a door. The bottom half of the door was wood, and the top was glass. Through the glass I saw SS officers, men, just looking through and laughing. I felt so terribly embarrassed. I wanted to get away, but I couldn't go anywhere. Still, the showers didn't come on, so they sent us out to sit on benches and wait. Finally, they came back and said, "OK, get out and put something on." The clothes were all in a big pile. People just grabbed anything. Then we were sent back to our cell.

I always thought the shower didn't work. But today, after more than 60 years, I believe it was the gas chamber that didn't work that day. They had never let us have a shower before. I was so lucky. But I didn't feel lucky… I wanted to die. I wanted it all to end. I didn't know anyone. I was alone. We didn't talk to one another. I had no parents or relatives or friends with me. I just wanted to die.

There had been another time I wanted to die. One day, we were marching in a line past a window, and I saw a jar of liquid sitting on the outside windowsill. I don't know what made me do it, but I grabbed that jar and took a drink. Did I think it was water? I don't know, but after one swallow, I dropped it. It burned my mouth and stomach. My stomach hurt so much, and I had nowhere to go. No one to care. No doctors. I just wanted to die. To this day, there is occasionally a smell I get from cleaning fluid, and that memory of how much my stomach hurt and how much I wanted to die when that happened comes back.

The Rescue

By this time, I was beginning to understand that this small place of confinement was a holding room before they killed us. We didn't know about the gas chambers then. But some days, there was a bad smell in the air like burned skin. Did I know what burned skin smelled like then? Or does that explanation come later after I learned what had happened? I don't know what we thought. Can you even think when you are that starved? We certainly were of no practical use anymore. Every day we faced only starvation and despair. And we were always covered in lice. Yet, we waited. For what? Food? Rescue? Death?

I dreamed that it would all just be over, and I'd be with Mama and Papa, and I'd tell Papa everything that had happened and what I had seen, and he would believe me. But then, how would anyone ever believe this? And then I would remember. Papa had died in that camp. And my sick Mama had been thrown off the train.

I now know and understand that killing massive numbers of people takes time. Imagine killing 6 million people! They were gassed. Then the bodies had to be removed and cremated. Then the furnaces had to be cleaned out. It took time. So we waited. But for what? Death? Rescue? I don't even think our minds could have been working very well we were so starved.

In the cell where we waited, I could see a very small piece of sky. That sky was my hope. My connection with a life I had once known. One day while standing there looking up at that sky, the door to the room opened, and the SS woman guard called out, "Valia Kopytina." I just assumed it was my time for the execution. A large woman was standing in the wide, dark hall outside our door. I walked over ready to go. I went into the hall and down at the end of that darkness I could make out the German soldier from perhaps a year before who said he would try to get me out of this. I saw his arm was missing. I knew it was him. He was talking to this guard, and I could tell by his hand movements and the way he was pointing, he was saying, "That's not her." Remember, I understood German, so I called out in German, "Yes, it is me. I AM the one you are looking for."

They both turned and walked away, and I stood there. I don't know how long I stood there alone and waiting, but eventually, he came back and got me. I don't remember how we left. I know he took me to a house where there were clothes and shoes and a scarf for my head. He told me to get dressed. It must have been there that he gave me a new identity.

"You are now Ledia Kleinburn. She is a real person who lost her life." He gave me her passport. "She was born in Kiev as you were, but to German parents. You must remember all this. Never ever tell anyone how you got this identity, or they will execute me first, and then you."

He took me to a railroad station and bought a ticket for me. The station was crowded with soldiers. "Now, get on the train and don't get off until the end of the journey. The conductor will come and tell you when it is at the end."

I must have fallen asleep. A man came to me and said, "This is the end. Get off here." I don't recall any other words. It was dusk when I got off the train. I saw no one and didn't know where I was. There was a road. A country road, just gravel and dirt, and it went over a bridge. I walked to the bridge and looked over the side. The river was raging. I stood there watching the power of the water in one spot where it must have been going over a big rock. I focused on that. I was in a trance it seemed, looking at it. I couldn't swim. There was no one around, and no one to miss me. I was tired, hungry, dirty, alone, and frightened. I remember thinking that I could just end it right here. I thought it would be quick. No one was around to see me, and no one would miss me.

I was watching that water thinking of ending it all right there . . . when someone tapped me on the shoulder. It was a large lady in a uniform wearing some pin on her coat. She just said, "Come with me," and she kept walking. We didn't walk far until we came to a house. A fence with a small gate to walk through was by it. The gate had a clicking sound when it moved. What a thing to remember! She had a key to the house. She opened it, and we went inside. I guess she knew I had been in prison by the looks of my hair and my body. She was very businesslike. "Take a bath," she ordered. At least it sounded like an order.

At my healthiest, I was only five feet tall, and given only a minimal diet, I must have weighed less than 60 or 70 pounds at that time. I was covered in lice. It was in my hair. It was in my underwear. That was the first hot water I had been in for at least 9 months! I can't describe how good it felt. When she came to get me, she asked in a very matter-of-fact tone, "Have you done something drastic to be in prison?"

"No. I was there by mistake."

I learned she was head of the German Red Cross. She put me in a room by myself with a bed. It had two down pillows and a down cover. I could not grasp the changes that had happened to me in just this one day.

The next morning, the Red Cross lady took me to work with her and talked to me about my future. She wanted to know what I had wanted to do or be before I was captured. I told her that I had always wanted to be a doctor of children, a pediatrician. She said that they could train me to be a nurse, and I could work for the German army.

That was my choice. I had no other. Nothing. I had nowhere else to go. I had this opportunity to live, and in doing so, I might someday find Mama and Papa. I had continued to waiver between believing they too had survived and the certainty they were dead. She said they would provide my clothes, food, lodging, and training to be a war nurse.

I was now 17 years old.

Training for War Nurses

When I think back about it now, about what happened next, I remember I was trained to be a war nurse, but before that happened, I must have been somewhere to get healthier. I could not have gone straight into training. It must have been some days or weeks later, I really don't know. I boarded a train with an older woman who was going with me for this special training to become war nurses. The training was maybe 3 months long. That's all. I remember that the older woman with me didn't pass a test for something like how to properly bandage a head wound. I was so surprised that she failed the test, and I passed.

Remembering bandages brings back another memory. I was sewing myself a bra. I don't believe I had ever had one. It must have been here when I had some bandages I decided I could make myself one. I had always watched Mama sew.

The medical training was a quick course in first aid, injections, bandages, etc. I can tell you that it was nothing like the training I later received on the job. Then I was doing things like administering ether during surgery. That scares me even now to think about it, and every time that memory comes to mind, I am so thankful that no one died while I was doing that. Later, when I was working as a nurse in America, I learned that the nurses here were not doing the kinds of things I had been doing on the battlefield in World War II, even though they had much more training.

They didn't send me to battlefields straight from this training. They first sent me to a Polish labor camp. I was working there, and I had my own very small room. It was small, but it had a little bed, a little table, and it had a small window. I don't remember anyone sharing that room with me.

A tall wire fence surrounded the camp, and German soldiers guarded it all the time. I had to keep reminding myself that I was *not* the prisoner, and I could not, should not, act like a prisoner. I could not show any fear, which I had, of these German guards.

I was free to wander around the camp but not to leave the camp. I was not to socialize at all with any of the prisoners. But there was a woman prisoner in the camp who had a little girl. The little girl was just learning to walk. It was very unusual to see a child. I don't remember ever seeing another child in a camp. When I would go to the place somewhat like a cafeteria where we were given something to eat, I would ask to take my food back to my room. But instead of going to my room, I would try to find this woman and her little girl so I could give the food to them. I knew it was dangerous and I better not get caught giving them food. I never was caught.

In this camp, I was in charge of a barrack full of women. The barrack was very long but not wide. It was made of wood. It was only boards nailed together. There was no insulation. It had a wooden floor, but it was not tightly sealed together. There were holes in the wood and space between the boards. A row of bunks was down each side of the barrack, and they were three bunks high. I remember that the one on the bottom almost touched the floor, and the one on the top almost touched the ceiling.

Everyone in this barrack had to go to work, and it was my duty to make sure they did. Then every day, I had to give a report that everyone in my barrack had reported to work.

The women would get up in the morning and be loaded into wooden carts pulled by horses and taken, it seems to me, to fields to work. They had to go, rain or shine. I never actually saw where they worked, but I must have heard them talking about the fields.

One day, an old woman told me she could not go to work. I remember her well. She was on one of the lower beds. Another woman was across the room. I looked at them and talked to them awhile, and I believed they were indeed too sick to work.

It was my job to report to the guard every day that my barrack was empty. I remember the day I had to report to this guard. He was a very handsome man. He had sharp features, dark hair, and dark eyebrows. He was tall, and he stood so straight. He wore tall, black boots that came up almost to his knees. So, on that day, I told him that two women stayed in the barrack because they were too sick to work.

The next thing I know, he pulled out this knuppel and said, "Here, take this. This will make them work." He was serious, and he was very angry and demanded that I hit these women with the whip.

I was outraged, and without thinking, I exploded at him, "I won't do it!"

He was speechless with rage that I had spoken to him in such a manner, so he put me under house arrest. I could have jumped out the window in my room, but where would I have gone? I couldn't escape.

Next thing I remember, I saw a man with a large briefcase walking to my room. I was left alone with him, and I told him the truth of what happened. I told him I could not beat sick, old women. He seemed sympathetic to what I was telling him.

He said they would take me to the Hauptstelle (Red Cross administrative building), but we had to take the train to get there, and I needed to pack my things. There wasn't much to pack.

When we arrived at the Red Cross building, he went inside to talk to an older nurse. They had me wait in a surgery room. I was told I could lie on the exam bed and sleep if I wanted. So I did.

The war was going on outside the window. I heard explosions, bombings, and guns were being shot. When they came back into the room, the man said, "I have more important things to do. I'm going to leave you here."

I don't know where I stayed that night, but the next morning, the nurse came to me and said, "I can give you two choices. There is a great need for nurses on the front lines, or you can go back to a labor camp."

At that moment of choice, I didn't even care. I told her I would go to the front. To work on the front was a voluntary job. Most nurses preferred to work in field hospitals. A few times during the war, some would come to the front, but they didn't last a day.

I was always scared of being caught. They thought I was Ledia Kleinburn—a German war nurse. What would they have done to me if they found out who I *really* was? What would happen if they learned I was really a Russian prisoner? I thought it would be easier for me to hide on the front.

So, that is where they put me. I worked with a medic team headed up by a Doctor Frank, who was an American. The memories from here are scattered. On the front, we rarely had any time to rest. It was daily, nonstop, high drama work. We were patching up soldiers and helping some die, all while we were also dodging bullets and working without needed supplies. We were scared we were going to die, and sometimes, I just wanted to die. It seems that during this time, I never slept.

So the memories that come from this time of the war are somewhat as scattered, as I guess, we were. I am not sure of the order. Most of the time, we didn't even know what country we were in. And, of course, when we were fighting the Russians, I had to remember I was working as a German.

I was assigned to a medical unit that was headed by Doctor Frank. Everyone else working there had volunteered, just like I had. I, or perhaps all of us, was never exactly sure where our location was. We just went where we learned we were most needed. We moved around in a bus and set up camp.

CHAPTER 3

Memories From The Front

Cross

WE WERE IN a village, and there was a fire inside a barn and a fire outside. A woman came running toward us who had a cross. It was a somewhat small metal cross like for a necklace, but it was not on a chain. It was on cloth like a rag. She gave it to me but said nothing. Then she turned and ran away. I didn't have time then to think about what it meant and why she did that. But even then, I knew it was brave of her, and I believed it was something like protection she wanted to give to me . . . or to all of us.

Lice

Just as in Auschwitz, everyone had lice. Not just the soldiers. Lice were everywhere. It was in my hair. It was in my underwear. We'd put arm or leg casts on lots of the soldiers, and the lice would get under there and eat at the flesh. They would beg for a stick or something to scratch under their cast.

Once I got hold of a little gasoline, thinking I would try to put some on my hair and maybe that would kill them. It didn't. But even if it had, I guess they would have been right back the next day.

Uniforms and a Photo

Someone must have washed our uniforms. I don't remember having any money to pay someone to do it. I never remember doing it myself.

But one day, I do remember that I was in my uniform and walking through a little village. There was a woman with a small child standing on the street with a shallow, woven basket of violets, and I bought some from her. I love flowers. I did then, and I do now.

So I was walking down the street holding onto my small bouquet when I saw a photography studio, and I thought, "Why not get a picture of myself?" The photographer had me take my nurse's cap off. Then he pulled the apron straps off my shoulder and draped a scarf around me, and pinned those violets on me. I brought that photo to the States with me, but now it is missing.

The Downed Russian Pilot

We were working out of a schoolhouse. The war was going on around us when a Russian plane was shot down by the Germans. They brought the pilot in. He was walking, but his face was swollen like a balloon, and his hands had not been protected from the fire. I told the doctor I would take care of him.

"No, Ledia," he told me, "we have to take care of our own first."

I thought . . . "He IS my own."

Later, when I had a chance to take care of him, I spoke to him in Russian. He was surprised. He asked me if I was Russian, and I told him I was. He needed to go to the bathroom, and his eyes were swollen shut, so I took him outside to an area where he could go. The Russian army was very near. I showed him how to get down to the ground and which direction to crawl to, to get back to the Russian troops.

One might wonder if I thought about defecting while I had a chance. But I had on a German uniform. Would they believe me? My greatest fear, more than dying, was the Germans finding out I was really a Russian, and the Russians believing that I was really German.

Bandages

As a nurse with little formal training, I learned to do so many things. During the war, I did labs, X-rays, gave injections, helped with surgeries, and even gave the anesthesia. I was used to being in charge and making quick decisions, big decisions, and I was very sure of myself. But then at night I would think through the day and worry I might have been wrong. But I never lost anyone. Maybe they died from some other cause, but not while I was helping them.

No matter how confident or capable I was, or any of us were, we could never get enough bandages. One day we were out, and we needed them so badly. That night, Doctor Frank told me and the medic working with us to go into town and break into the pharmacy and get bandages. We did it, but there weren't many. Another time, we broke into an empty house and found sheets. We took them all and had the patients who were able to help tear them into strips and roll them up into bandages.

Another day, someone drove up in something which looked like a Red Cross ambulance and unloaded boxes and boxes full of bandages. We were so excited! When we opened the first box, I noticed how tightly and evenly they were rolled. But it turned out to be white crepe paper! We tried using it. It was nice the way it stretched into any position, but it would not hold blood. They were worthless.

I did find a little use for them, though. At the time, I was living in a tent with three other nurses. I always tried as best I could to make where I lived to feel like a home. Just a little thing could help. So I took that white crepe paper and strung it up to look like curtains. The other girls thought I was crazy, but I liked it.

New Nurses

Doctor Frank said we were getting some new nurses on the front to help us. He left to get them, even though enemy fire was going on all around. Injured soldiers were everywhere, all lined up, and there was more live fire coming into the area when these nurses arrived. They saw what was happening . . . all the injured, all the shooting— and they immediately turned around and left. We didn't have anyone in charge. We just moved around wherever we were needed, but we could never keep up. Red Cross nurses did not have to stay on the front lines unless they chose to. Most stayed in field hospitals behind the front lines.

The Ring

We traveled around in an old bus sometimes. We had buses and trucks. They all had the German Red Cross symbol painted on them, on the top and the sides. It didn't seem to matter, though. It seemed we got shot at just as much as anyone else. I was traveling on the bus with Doctor Frank and another guy, and I had fallen asleep. I woke up when the bus stopped. I looked out the window and could see Doctor Frank's back as he walked down the road. He was a very tall man, about six foot five. He was a good man, a kind and gentle man. I liked working with him.

As I became more awake, I realized we must be at a town where we had heard there was a sniper. A soldier came running toward the bus yelling, "Doctor Frank is dead. Doctor Frank is dead."

I jumped out of my seat and began giving orders. "Get a tent." We needed something to carry him on, and all our medical supplies were in another truck that hadn't arrived yet. So one of the young soldiers grabbed a tent, and we ran to get him. We made a stretcher out of the tent, put him on it, and began pulling him back. I don't know how I did that. I was five foot one and weighed less than 100 pounds.

He was dead. We pulled him into the village. We needed to get out of there, but we couldn't just leave him. The war was raging all around us. Guns and bombs were exploding all over. While running to get him, I had seen this huge hole. It was as long as a house but not very wide. Somehow, I knew it was a grave. A man was standing there that looked like a religious man. He stood by this hole and had a book in his hand. He didn't wear robes, but he had this thing like a very long shawl hanging around his neck and down in the front.

We pulled Doctor Frank to this hole. It was full of bodies. Dead people were all lined up in that hole. It seemed like it was just men, probably soldiers.

We said, "Please let us bury this man." The priest, or whoever he was, said there was no more room. The hole was already filled to the top. They wanted to put some dirt over the bodies and say a prayer, and they needed to leave quickly. The soldier who was with me begged this religious man to let us bury Doctor Frank.

The priest then said, "OK, maybe if you get down in there and move some of the bodies closer together, we can get one more in." The soldier got into the hole and moved the bodies closer together, and Doctor Frank was put in at the end, but he was too long. He wouldn't fit. Someone handed the soldier a shovel, and he quickly dug out an area to make room for the doctor's feet and lower legs.

Before he got out of the hole, the soldier took Doctor Frank's hand and took off his wedding ring. Doctor Frank had not been married very long. He gave the ring to me and said, "After this war is over, find his wife and give it to her." There was no time in war to get acquainted personally. I didn't even remember his wife's name. I didn't know where he lived. I didn't even know Doctor Frank's first name. I had no idea how to get the ring to her. But I didn't have time to even think about it then. I must have kept it because I brought it with me to the United States and had it sized down. I wore it for many years; then I gave it to my granddaughter.

I was always telling myself, "When this war is over, I'm going to tell my father, and he'll fix it."   I still wanted to believe that my father was alive. It gave me strength.

The General

It was while I was working on the front lines that a rumor was going around that a nurse who had done something heroic was going to get a special honor. I didn't think it would be me, and I hoped it wouldn't be me. But an event had happened recently that made me wonder. Guns and bombs were going off all around us. I was on a roadside with other medical people. We saw a young German soldier get hit. He fell just on the other side of a wire fence. No one would do anything. I was frantic. "Isn't anybody going to get him?" I asked. "No" was all I heard. "You'd get killed going out there." I ran across the road anyway and got on my belly and crawled under the fence. I got to the soldier and said, "Pull your body over mine."

He was having too much trouble moving, so I slid my body under him and crawled back. We made it, and he got the care he needed. We moved on. Only later I would wonder, "How did I do that?" I was such a small person. But I didn't think; I just reacted. All I could see was a wounded boy who needed help, and I was just doing what needed to be done.

We just keep moving where the battles were. It was hard even to know what country we were in—Poland, Germany, Russia? Some days later, I really don't know how many, I saw a Jeep coming up with a German soldier driving. I thought a couple of other soldiers were in the Jeep. They wanted me to go with them. I was petrified I'd get caught. I was afraid they learned who I really was—a Russian, and they'd kill me. I hoped they'd just shoot me. I have seen killing in so many ways, and I decided I'd rather just be shot, so that's what I hoped they would do to me.

They did not seem angry or ready to fight. They put a big army coat around me, and I climbed into the Jeep. I was still so scared, but I was resigned to dying. I must have fallen asleep. The next thing

49

I remembered, I was brought into a room. On my left was a man, perhaps the age of my grandfather, sitting in a rocking chair. He had a big belly and on his lap sat a little dachshund. It was all so civilized and natural looking. It was also disorienting. It was so out of place in the midst of this war. The way others were treating him, I assumed he was the highest ranking officer around.

He said to me, "It is a special day for our soldiers and others like you who have supported our troops. Tonight, we will have a movie. We have a room and a bed for you to rest in before this evening's activities. Set your boots outside the door of your room. They will be cleaned, and we'll come and get you later."

I was taken to a room, and the first thing I saw was white sheets. You can't imagine how beautiful those white sheets looked. And a bed. A real bed! How long had it been since I had slept in a real bed with clean, white sheets? I put my boots outside the door as he had told me to do. I was not sure why, but I was more concerned about washing up and going to bed. Once I lay down, I was out like a light.

When I woke up, I opened the door . . . and there sat my boots shining more than I ever believed could be possible.

Later, an officer came to escort me to a meeting. He had on a dress uniform. I remember on the shoulders of his coat were shoulder boards with gold fringe hanging off all around them. I don't know what I was wearing. Surely, they had brought me clean clothes. He took me to a large room with maybe 100 soldiers in it, and they stood and clapped and whistled when we walked in. We watched a movie. I don't remember what else happened.

I don't remember the food, what the movie was about, or why I was invited to be there. But the general gave me a picture of himself and signed it. I brought it with me to this country, and somewhere along the way, in all my moves, I guess I must have lost it.

CHAPTER 4

War Seems to be Ending

Two Boys

MEMORIES BECAME CHAOTIC as the war was ending. Everything was chaotic. Where were we? Where was I going? Who was in charge? Was *anybody* in charge?

The war was still going on, but it must be very close to the end. The Russians were taking over where we were, and we, the Germans, were trying to pull away. The Russians were so close I could see them running in the distance.

It was late in the day, soon to be dark. Some German soldiers came up with two short Russian prisoners, probably not more than 15 or 16 years old. They were wearing oversized coats that hung to the ground. They were scared. The German soldiers threw these two young Russian boys in a shed and locked the door. I saw where they put the key.

I had just received orders to leave with two German officers who had very serious wounds. Everyone was trying to get out of there before the Russians arrived.

I saw an opportunity when no one was watching, and I took the key to the shed and opened the door. I was shocked to see how young they looked. I started talking to them in Russian, and they began crying. "We are not soldiers. We just cook for them."

"Your brothers are over there." I pointed in the direction they needed to go. "Get down on your bellies and start crawling, and you can get to them." When it seemed no one was watching, I told them to go. Then I locked the shed and put the key back. I was in a big hurry because I had two wounded officers, and I had to get help for them.

Overhead, I heard a plane that sounded like it was flying low. I fell on the ground and looked up. It was a very small Russian plane with room for only one. It flew so low and fast. I saw a guy holding a gun that was attached to the airplane, and it was pointed at me. He was so close we could look into each other's eyes. He didn't fire.

The Horse & Cart

I immediately went to the wounded German officers. I had been ordered to take them somewhere for help. The officers were placed in a wooden cart that had large wooden wheels on the sides, and the cart was hitched to a big horse. I had never ridden on a horse or driven a horse cart. I climbed up onto the cart seat and held onto the reins and the whip, wondering what I was supposed to do. They handed me a *knuppel* (whip) and slapped the horse and told it to go.

The horse started walking and just kept walking. We came to an area where there were trees on the right, and everything else was snow. When we got past the forest, I heard a rapid *boom, boom, boom,* and saw Russian tanks coming toward us. Not on the road, but coming in our direction across the land. Fire was going on all around us, but that horse just kept on walking.

I was so scared. As with so many things in the war, I just acted and reacted. I did what I thought had to be done at the moment. But now, the course of the war was changing. No one seemed to be in charge. The Russians were moving in, which gave me a little hope. I was responsible for helping the two Russian boys, but I'm working for the Germans. It was now dark, and I was scared of the horse. But everything was so white with snow, that it was light enough to see.

Up ahead I could make out a foot bridge. It didn't look wide enough for the cart to get across. And if it was a bridge, then what was under it? Was there water? Ice? I knew this was the way these German officers and I would die. I had no idea how to control the horse that just kept moving toward the bridge.

To make it worse, on the other side of the bridge was fire. Something was burning, and that horse just kept walking. I had heard that horses were afraid of fire and would run away. I remember the *klump, klump, klump* of those cart wheels as they kept turning, and we kept moving toward that foot bridge and the fire. That horse just kept going, across the bridge and past the fire without ever changing its pace.

Eventually, the horse and I got the soldiers where they were supposed to go. I was so scared and exhausted. I imagine we went to another field hospital, and they probably gave me food, and then I fell asleep.

First Plane Ride

After that horse ride with the wounded soldiers, I was told to board an aircraft loaded with wounded soldiers. It was my first time on an airplane. The pilot asked me to come to the cockpit. I went in and saw all those instruments and the panels of glass windows in front of us. He closed the door to the cockpit, and a small seat with a strap across it folded down from that door. He told me to take that seat and secure the straps over me.

It was dark outside. "How do you know where you are going in the dark?" "See that star out there? I know how to follow it." We took off.

I don't remember how I felt about that first airplane ride because very quickly, we were distracted by an attack from below. I looked out and saw balls and balls of fire in the sky.

"Don't worry; just concentrate. We'll get out of here."

What did I do? Pass out? Fall asleep? Was I fascinated or terrified? I can't remember, and I don't know where we landed.

War Ending

When the war was finally ending, I was working in a field hospital in a building which I think was a deserted schoolhouse. People outside began yelling, "The war is over! The war is over!" Some of the soldiers were very happy, and others were shouting, "No, we will fight. No, it is *not* over."

The soldiers lying around were scared of what would happen to them. They didn't want me to leave. I was not sure what to do. Could I really just leave? Could I leave these boys and men? There weren't many women around during the war, and I think those boys were comforted by a woman's presence. I cared about them. I cared deeply. But how could I tell each one good-bye? Was I free? Was I really free to be free?

I fought with the decision for only a short time, and then I just started walking off the floor and out of the building. Many were calling to me, "Don't leave, Nurse. Stay." I couldn't say good-bye to everyone. That was so hard for me. As much as I wanted this war to be over, it was so hard to walk out on those boys. But I walked anyway. I just walked away with tears in my eyes, and I didn't look back.

Outside, soldiers were yelling "Put your guns in a pile." Some of the guys wouldn't do it.

Everyone was free; chaos was everywhere. War was always chaos, but this was worse. We were free to do whatever we wanted, but we didn't even know where we were. Was this Poland? Was it Russia? Some of the soldiers outside were looking at a map trying to figure it out.

I wanted to go back to Russia, but I had no Russian ID anymore. I didn't think my parents would be there anyway. And if they were, and if I went back with a history of working for Germany, I would just be killed. Killed! In my own country. I didn't know what to do. Where should I go?

I joined up with a group of soldiers who were walking. I walked for miles, but I couldn't keep up because of my feet. They were blistered and hurting badly, and I couldn't keep up with them, so I stopped and rested, and they kept going. Eventually, I started walking again by myself. I came to a farmhouse and asked a woman if I could rest. She took me to the barn and brought me a kettle of water so I could wash and soak my feet. It felt so good. She also brought me a blanket and some food.

The next day, I was walking up a hill. Soldiers were scattered around here and there, and I learned that some Americans were farther up the hill. I had never seen American soldiers. I didn't care that they were American, I was just afraid to run into Russians.

I started up the hill that had woods and forests along the side. I saw a Jeep coming down the hill; it was not on the road but swerving in and out of the trees. As it got closer, I could see the driver. He was black. I'd never seen a black person before, so I thought he must be very, very dirty from the war. I could tell he was trying to drive closer to me.

People were scattered all over the hill. He drove over to me and started speaking English. I could not understand him, so he pointed for me to get into his Jeep. He pulled out a gun and pointed it at me to get into the Jeep.

By this time, two German soldiers had caught up with me and saw what was happening. They said, "She's a nurse." Nurses were very respected by the Germans. This black man said, "But she's a woman."

I thought, so this is what Americans are like. I had been afraid of getting caught by the Germans for being Russian and caught by the Russians for working for Germany, and now this American is up to no good. I was afraid, and I didn't trust anybody.

I finally made it up to the top of the hill. I had been told American nurses were supposed to be down the hill on the other side. That was where I was trying to get to. A very young white American soldier saw me and came over. I thought that he was trying to help me get to the American nurses.

I was wearing an inexpensive nurse's watch and a little necklace of no value to anyone else. The young soldier was angry and pointing to the watch and necklace for me to take them off. I wouldn't, so he grabbed the necklace and ripped it off and motioned me to go on.

I went a few steps, then another American soldier came up on a horse and spoke to me in German. By this time, I was in tears and full of fear. I thought the war was over, yet there was still no safe place.

I was crying and telling him in German about the boy who took my jewelry, and he spoke to me in English. He rode after the boy. He told the thief to open his coat, and when he did, it was lined with pockets. He ordered him to empty the pockets. They were loaded with watches and other jewelry. He found a watch and handed it to me and said, "Here, take this one. It is the best."

By this time, I was afraid to go to the American nurses down the hill. I was afraid of Americans, so I got back on the road and started walking again.

An American Jeep drove by and passed me on the left, but it stopped and backed up. They asked me in English, "Do you speak English?" I had never heard English, and I couldn't speak it then. So he asked, "Polish? Russian?" I was afraid to speak Russian, so I said in Polish that I speak some Polish. They were going to the border of Russian occupation where they would change guards. "The ones we change with will be coming back. You stay here. Go with them when they return. They are good. Don't be afraid." He wanted me to wait, and he gave me a bottle of Coke and a ration box.

I gobbled up the food in that ration box. I was so hungry. I didn't know when I had last eaten, but the food made me thirsty. The Coke bottle had a metal cap on it, and I hadn't seen that before. I couldn't figure out how to open it, so I started beating the bottle cap on a tree. I beat it and beat it until the cap popped off and started to spew everywhere. A memory flashed back at me. I had heard about champagne and its bubbles. I think Mama had told me about it, and she said never to drink it. I was convinced they were trying to get me drunk, so I couldn't trust these soldiers either.

Then I saw the military truck coming down the road, the one

that I was told I could trust. They stopped and offered me the ride. I was afraid, but I was so tired and thirsty. They said, "We'll take you to the hospital in Passau, Germany." It is located in the Black Forest. I went along with them, and we arrived during the night. It seemed we were entering a base. Someone was trying to explain who I was.

Passau, Germany

They put me in a nice apartment in a woman's house. I was able to take a real bath. I was given a nightgown to wear. It was over-sized. The woman had a daughter called Pia. Pia was not home so I was told to take her room. This woman's husband was a prisoner of war. That night, I had the first real food, bath, and bed that I had had in a very long time.

I had seen there was a key in the lock on the hallway side of the door. I took it out and brought it into the room and locked the door from the inside. Around midnight, I heard heavy boot steps coming down the hall, and they stopped at my door. When I heard those boots, I had flashbacks of that sound outside the walls of our room when I was in Russia before we were rounded up. I'd hear the sound of those steps at night, and the next morning, people we knew would be gone. As a child, I had such fear that one day they would come and take my papa away. So now, I heard this sound again, and a male voice said, "Open up."

I refused. I kept quiet. I saw that the window opened onto the fire escape and a balcony. I grabbed a coat to put over my night-gown and climbed out the window onto the balcony and started down the fire escape. I went to the guard house and told them what had happened. They started laughing at me and told me I could go back. They escorted me back to the house. As I went in, I walked quietly down the hall past this woman's room. The door to her room was open a little, and I could see her in bed with *two men!* In spite of all I had seen in war, this was most shocking.

I wanted out of there. The next day, I was taken to a German hospital run by Americans. There were so many wounded German soldiers; the wards were filled to overflowing.

One day, I was told that an American doctor was coming to work in our hospital. When he arrived, I saw he was young and good looking. However, any uninjured and clean young man looked good then. He seemed to have an eye for me, but I avoided him except in our work. He had an interpreter who worked with him.

One day I came into the hospital, and it smelled like chocolate. It took awhile to remember what that smell was because it had been so long. Chocolate. I could smell it and see it in my mind. I salivated. I wondered where it was. I wanted some.

This young doctor used the interpreter to tell me that he had ordered the nuns to bake a chocolate cake. Later, he slipped a note into my pocket. He couldn't speak or write in German, but the paper had only two words he tried to sound out by writing "KOMM" and "KAK." I knew what he meant, and I was going to get me some of that chocolate cake no matter what his intentions might have been.

Every day after lunch, I had the patients in the ward take a nap. Well, they rarely ever really napped, but it was a quiet time, and it was a break from medical care. They could rest and talk with each other while medical personnel took a break. We also could rest and talk with each other.

This seemed like a good time for me to go to the doctor's room. I knocked on the door, and he opened it. I saw the cake sitting on his desk. I had not had cake or chocolate in 6 years. He gave me a piece, and I bit into a little bit of happiness. But by the time I was taking my second bite, there was a loud knock on his door. I wrapped the cake in a napkin because I was not about to leave it. He sent me out a back door in his room. It was dark when I opened this door, and I didn't know where it went. After my eyes adjusted, I could see I was in the quarters where the nuns lived. It was like a ward itself, with each nun's bed and table separated by curtains. I looked around and found another door that came out into a hallway that I recognized. From there, I knew how to get to my own room, where I went and finished my cake and then went back to work. I don't have more memories of that doctor, but I sure do remember the cake and the chocolate.

A Love Story

I am reluctant to tell this story, but much time has passed, and my children are grown, and I am now a widow, so I will tell this much. There was an American doctor who came to oversee the German hospital and work with the German doctors. I think he had a higher rank than the "Chocolate Doctor" because he had private quarters. He was married. At first, we just had a good working relationship, and then it seemed like we were friends. Our good friendship evolved into a romantic attraction. I never asked anything of him, nor expected anything. He made it clear he was going back to his wife. The first and the last time I had been with a man until I met him had been when the Nazis used me.

With him, it was so different. He healed me. He gave me the understanding of what it was like to be wanted and to want. I loved him for that, and I believed we loved each other, even knowing it was a relationship that wouldn't last. That's really all I need to say about it. The memory of him has lived in my heart with deep love and appreciation. It made it possible for me to love a man later when I came to this country.

From Passau to Portland

I had been working in Passau, Germany, in a hospital run by Americans. Not long after the war ended, I wanted my Russian name back. I didn't want to tell any details. I just told them I had been captured and then rescued. I said that all my identity had been lost, and I had nothing to prove who I was, where I was born, or how old I was. I said that my name had been changed, and I just wanted my birth name back.

This happened to many people during the war, and there was a lot of sympathy for people in this situation. But to get it back, I had to have three witnesses who would swear I was who I said I was since I had no papers to prove anything.

I had some people who would not swear they had known me, but they spoke to my character and made it clear that I had worked as a nurse for the German army during the war.

Maybe this guy just thought that since I had worked for their country, he would give me the necessary papers I needed. Why he did it, I don't really know or care, but I was so glad to be free of Ledia Kleinburn (or to let Ledia Kleinburn be free of me) and to be Valia Kopytina again.

Word was floating around that many countries, including France, England, Germany, and the United States of America, had a short-age of nurses, and they were looking for war nurses to come to their countries.

The news was that Stalin was asking his people to come back. "Come back, my people. I will give you a roof over your head and food to eat." It sounded good, but I didn't believe it, and I had no people to go back to. I was tired of all the ruins. Cities everywhere were destroyed. Food was in short supply everywhere.

Germany was not a bad country, but I knew I did not want to stay there. I had too many bad memories of what had happened to me during the war. I wanted to go where there were no visual effects of war. I wanted to go where food was plentiful. I chose America be-cause it had not been destroyed by World War II. I gathered together all my papers and my newly recovered Russian identity; then I went to this beautiful building in Passau, Germany. Such a beautiful town it was. There were pockets of beauty that remained after the war. In Passau, no buildings had been destroyed, and they still had electricity and water.

I talked with a woman and told her that I had no family and I did not want to return to Russia or to stay in Germany. She said that I would be a perfect candidate. Then she asked if I spoke English. My heart sank. "No, I speak Russian, German, and Polish but no English."

She said, "We have another ship leaving for America in 6 months. You will need to learn enough English to be able to go."

"I can do it," I told her without having any idea how I would go about learning English when there were no schools to attend and no books to read. She just looked at me in disbelief, but the challenge was mine. Germany had lost the war, and the Americans were running their hospitals. There were not good feelings about that. I had to be very neutral as I went about learning English.

Erica and Strupy

At this time, I was living in a small room with Erica, a German nurse, and her dog, Strupy. Can you believe she had a dog? Not enough food for the two of us, yet we had a dog to feed! But Erica also had an American boyfriend who was willing to help me as he could, and we began keeping anything of his that had English words on it. I also would pick pieces of paper off the ground looking for English words.

Erica was something else. She was much more willing to do things than I was, but sometimes, I let her talk me into joining her activities. The only clothes we owned were our nurses' uniforms. We had three. First, we had a navy-blue suit that was our dress uniform. Then we had two dresses for the nurse's uniform. One was blue and the other blue striped. We had a separate attached white collar that was something like plastic which was held together with our Red Cross pin. We could take the collar off and wash it separately. We had two white aprons to go over the dress. We also wore a white nurse's cap when we were working. The cap fit around the entire back of our head and held tight with elastic. All of our hair had to be inside the cap. Our shoes were black with laces. We wore white stockings. These were the only clothes we had.

When we were not working, we took off the cap, collar, and sometimes the stockings. One day, Erica's American boyfriend said there was going to be a party at the military club, and Erica wanted me to go along. I had no idea how we were possibly going to dress to go to a party. Erica came up with a long strip of colorful fabric. She ripped it down the length and had two long scarves. We took off our aprons, and she wrapped that scarf around the waist of our dresses. Then she turned our collars under and left the top button or two undone . . . and there we were. She had made us ready for a U.S. military party.

Another day, she decided she wanted to get apples from a nearby apple orchard. The orchard was completely fenced in, but she had found a place we could crawl under and get inside to get an apple. She said these were the best apples she had ever tasted.

I said, "This is stealing. We can't do it." But I let her talk me into it. Around dusk, I went with her, and we managed to crawl under that fence with Strupy along with us. But as soon as we had gotten under that fence, we heard gunshots. Someone was shooting at us! I couldn't believe I could die in an apple orchard after surviving the war!

"I've got to get an apple," she insisted. "I'm out of here," I said. Shots fired again, and we got under that fence with Strupy with us. Suddenly, she stood up laughing and laughing and held up two apples.

And, yes, they really were good.

All this time I was trying to learn English. I'd figured out the alphabet, and by sounding out words, I was learning to spell and read basic things. So after my 6 months were up, I went back to the Red Cross headquarters in Passau and took the English test. I have to tell you I just barely squeaked by. She wanted to know where in America I wanted to go. I was so tired of cold and snow. I had been told there was a place in America where the grass was green, even at Christmas. It was called Portland, Oregon. I had no idea where that was, but I told her that was where I wanted to go.

The ship had already left, but she said there was a military flight leaving. I packed quickly, which couldn't have taken very long since I had so little. I got on the flight, and we left from Frankfurt and made a stop in Greenland for refueling. I will never forget how barren and white Greenland was. From Greenland, we went to New York. I came by bus from New York to Portland, Oregon. I don't remember having any money for that trip, but surely the Red Cross had given me a little. I arrived at the bus depot in the winter of 1947. We had a winter storm in December 2008; the news said it was the worse one on record since the winter of 1947!

Two nurses from Emanuel Hospital School of Nursing met me at the bus depot. I was so tired and concerned about the snow. They told me it would go away in just a few more days. Sure enough, one morning as I was waking up in my dorm room, I heard water running. The head of my bed was next to the outside wall where the downspout was located. I looked out the window, and the snow was melting. In spots, I really could see green grass! It was a dream come true.

I had no money but was given uniforms, books, and my meals. Some weekends, the girls would go to a movie, and they would all pitch in a little for me so I could go along too.

Mrs. McFadden was a supervisor and teacher on the floor, and everyone said she could be so awful. But I remember her because she came to me and put her arm around me and said, "You do such a good job."

Doctor Brunkow taught classes in family practice. He knew that I was having such difficulty with the language and that I had no money, so he suggested I work for him for 5 to 12 months, and then it would be easier for me to go back and finish school. So I went to work for him and stayed for 27 years. I didn't want to leave. The Brunkows made me part of their family. He had a wife and three children, and they included me in their family activities.

After leaving nurses' training, I lived in a room of my own that was in the home of an elderly lady who lived in a very large house by herself. But I had no freedom there, and I couldn't use the kitchen. So eventually, I rented a room upstairs on SE Hawthrone, where I had a little kitchen, bath, bedroom, and sunroom. It was so small, but I had all those little spaces for myself.

Later, I shared that space with Marie. When she got married and had a little girl, she named her Vallie. I lived there until I married at 27.

Pigeons (on the Courthouse)

While I was going to nurses' training at Emanuel Hospital in NE Portland and working for Dr. Milton Brunkow in the Medical Arts Building in SW Portland, I also went to classes for citizenship. In the evenings after work, I would walk up the hill to Portland State University for classes. Then I would walk back toward the city again to catch a bus home to SE Portland.

Often, as I stood there across from the courthouse waiting to catch the bus, I would see these pigeons circling over the roof. It looked curious to me. Usually, it seemed to me pigeons hovered on the ground around people who were feeding them. These pigeons just circled, landed, flew up, and circled again. There must have been a hundred of them. You can see I had time just to watch and think as I waited for the bus. So I worked and studied very hard to learn English and some history of America to become a citizen. Maybe you understand now that you know my story. But how can anyone really understand who has not had their country, their parents, and nearly their own life ripped away?

I just wanted to become a citizen of this country and start all over. I studied all about the U.S. government, the role of senators, how laws are made, and stuff like that. We would be tested. If we couldn't answer the questions, we couldn't become a citizen. So one day, the teacher told us that our class was finished. She said that Judge McCollum would question us individually. She said he might look scary because he was a very big man and bald and serious and didn't smile much, but he really was nice, and we did not need to be afraid of him.

The day finally came for the exam, and I couldn't believe it when I walked to the courthouse and into the room where I was supposed to wait. The doctors and nurses were all there waiting for me, holding flowers.

I was led into an empty room by a receptionist and told to sit. It was a big room with one huge desk and two oversized leather chairs sitting in front of it. No one was in the room. I set my flowers on the desk and tried to sit in one of the chairs. They were so big. Three people my size could sit in them.

The door opened and in walked this giant man.

"What's that on my desk?"

My heart was racing, but I stammered, "Flowers."

"What are they doing here?"

"My friends gave them to me. The doctors and nurses I work with. They are sitting outside waiting for me."

After a pause and a grunt and no eye contact, he said, "OK, let's get going."

He proceeded to start asking questions I cannot remember anymore, but I got them all right. As he asked more and more questions, I kept getting them right, and I started relaxing more and felt very confident. Finally, he just stood up and said, "We're finished." He picked up his briefcase and threw his coat over his arm and started toward the door, but he stopped before he got there and said, "By the way, one more question. It's the last one but not the least."

I did not know what this "last but not least" meant, but he went on to ask me, "What is it we have flying over the courthouse?" and I just blurted out, "PIGEONS!" I felt so proud of myself.

He looked at me blankly. I think he tried to suppress a grin and just walked out the door. I heard him out there laughing. And before he had even made it to the door, I knew what I was supposed to say. I was devastated. I imagined being thrown on the next ship back to Russia. I had blown it. I would never become a citizen. It was over. How could I be so stupid?

I got up and walked out the door with my head down. The doctors and nurses were all waiting for me with big smiles. They had asked Judge McCollum how I did, and he had said, "She's a keeper."

The story didn't end there. Many years later, Doctor Brunkow was on vacation in Hawaii. He was in a restaurant and the waiter, who had learned where he was from, said to Doctor Brunkow, "Portland? Really? There is another man here from Portland. Perhaps you would like to meet him." So retired Judge McCollum came over, and the two men began to talk over drinks and more drinks and telling stories. Judge McCollum began to tell the story of this Greek girl who did so well in her exam, but when he asked what was flying over the courthouse, she had said "pigeons."

Doctor Brunkow knew this story, of course, and told him, "She wasn't Greek. That was Vallie. She's from Russia and worked for me. I was waiting in the hall for her afterward." Judge McCollum said that had always been the funniest story, and he had told it many times over the years.

Homicide

As you can imagine from my stories of being a nurse on the front lines of war in World War II, I was used to being in charge and just getting things done. I was also still learning English.

One day, I was the only nurse in Doctor Brunkow's office, though he also had a receptionist. The doctor was late getting to the office; the waiting room was filling up. In walks this man who didn't have an appointment but wanted to see Doctor Brunkow. I explained the delay, and he said he had paperwork that needed to be filled out regarding the death of Mrs. Ethel Johnson (name changed). Doctor Brunkow had called me earlier to tell me that by the time he got to Mrs. Johnson's house, she was dead. So I knew it was true. I really liked that woman and felt sad. I told this man that I would take the paperwork and fill it out so when the doctor came in, all he would have to do was just sign it. So I filled out the form, name, address, age, etc.

When Doctor Brunkow came back to the office, I handed him this form, and he read over every line, but at the bottom of the page, he paused and said, "What's this? I told you she was already dead when I got to her home."

"Yes, Doctor, but I had to check one of the boxes, and I knew she didn't kill herself, and I knew it wasn't an accident, and you said she died at home, so I checked Homicide."

I was so embarrassed and remained embarrassed for years as that story was told and retold. But now it is even funny to me.

Take a Douche

So many funny things happen with words when you are learning a new language. Let me clarify that there were two Doctor Brunkows. CW was the father who was soon to retire, and Michael was the son that I continued to work with for about 27 years. I had been working in Doctor Brunkow's office about a year when the following happened.

Doctor CW had a loyal receptionist who had been working with him for years and was going to continue with Doctor Michael. Her name was Louise. One day, she just casually asked me, "Vallie, what do you do in the evenings? Do you go to parties? Do you have friends you see?"

"No. By the time I work all day and go to school at night for my citizenship, I don't even cook. I just douche and go to bed."

So behind my back, she went to the doctor and said, "There's something strange about Vallie. I asked her what she does in the evenings and if she has friends, and she said that every night, she just takes a douche and goes to bed."

"Really? Maybe I can ask her about this. On the other hand, why don't you first ask again to make sure you heard her correctly?"

So Louise asked me a similar question again a few days later, and she got the same answer from me and told Doctor Brunkow.

So CW Brunkow came to me one day and asked me the same question about what I do in the evenings, and I told him the same thing I had told Louise.

"Let's talk about this, Vallie. Do you have problems?"

He went into his office and brought back a chart with pictures. "This is what a douche is in English."

I was so embarrassed. How was I to know that the word "shower" in Russian had a completely different meaning in English?

And, of course, they never forgot it. For years I would hear, "How was the douche last night? How's our douching nurse?"

Return to Russia, 1979

I did not return to Russia immediately after the war's end for a couple of reasons. The Russians were still in charge, I did not have a Russian passport, and I thought I would have been killed carrying German identification. I also had no reason to believe that my parents were still alive. I had seen my very ill Mama pushed off the train when we were first picked up, and Mama and I had been told that Papa was dead. Nevertheless, I felt a need to know for certain because Papa said we would all meet again there in Kiev after the war. It had remained a single thread of hope but a slim one. Furthermore, I had no reason to trust Stalin. He was still in power, and he had already been responsible for killing at least 20 million of his own people by starvation. And a sure death would have been guaranteed me by Stalin's government had they learned that I had worked for the German Red Cross during part of the war.

Communists were still in charge, so that meant that my trip was limited to traveling with the tour group that I had booked for myself. I chose this tour because it was scheduled to spend 2 days in Kiev. Those 2 days were all I really wanted. About 30 other people went along. My visa indicated that I was born in Kiev.

When we left Portland, Oregon, I was ready and feeling fine. We landed in Winnipeg, Canada, to change to the flight for Kiev. I was waiting to board when I looked out the window and saw two Russian military men in their uniforms standing by the plane that I was supposed to board. This was when you had to walk down across the tarmac to board a plane. I would have to walk right past those guards. I was overwhelmed with fear. I couldn't catch my breath. My heart was pounding out of my chest, and I was sweating and shaking. I told the flight personnel that I couldn't go on. I had made a mistake to come on this trip.

It turned out that a psychiatrist was in the group. He had already boarded, and they were waiting for me so the plane could leave. He came down the steps off the plane and onto the tarmac and back into the airport. I said, "I am not going. Just give me a ticket to go home."

He sat down next to me and talked. "What has upset you? You made these arrangements. Was it seeing those soldiers?"

I told him I was born in Russia. I realized now where I was going, and it was too dangerous. I shouldn't go. The more I talked and he listened and talked to me, the more I calmed down.

He convinced me to go on, took me by the hand, and walked me up the stairs. The attendants, all Russian girls, were standing at the door watching. I ended up becoming the interpreter for the group.

I had worked two jobs to save enough money to take this trip. In 1979, it cost me $3,200. That covered the 30-day trip but not any personal expenses. The trip was to cover all the Russian territories, but I was only really interested in those 2 days in Kiev. The Red Army was everywhere when we arrived, and it scared me so to see them.

We stayed in a big hotel in Kiev. We were not free to travel on our own into the city. I wanted to go back to the house where I was born. At one point, I left a walking tour we were on because I was only a couple of blocks from the house where I had lived with Mama and Papa. The rest of the tour was to visit a remarkable old Orthodox Christian church. But I had seen it many times thinking it was a museum.

I explained to the tour guide what I wanted to do. She begged me to hurry because they would not be able to wait for me. There was some risk involved because I would be outside the area we were to stay in. The building we had lived in was under reconstruction. When I looked up at the window where we had lived, the little girl inside me looked for Mama to smile and wave at me. But the only thing waving from that window was a shutter flapping in the breeze. I hurt all over. I cried.

I grabbed my camera to take a quick picture with my instamatic, and two young Russian policemen spotted me and yelled at me to stop. "Why?" I begged. "I was born here. This was my home." They told me I could come back and take the picture after the reconstruction. If I took the picture now, I would take it back to America and tell people this was what Russia looks like.

The only thing that remained alive which was part of my childhood was the giant tree outside the window. Half of it had broken off during the bombing, but a section remained alive, though it was growing off in a new direction. I went to the tree and wrapped my arms around it.

When we got back to the hotel, I got a phone call from a woman in the hotel office. She spoke to me in Russian. "Come down to the office. We want to ask you a couple of questions." I was so scared. I told my roommate where I was going in case I didn't come back.

I found the office and knocked on the door. A woman opened it, and I saw three women in the room and a pretty little table with a lace cloth over it. A *samovar* (teapot) was sitting on the table. They admired my fancy sunglasses and wanted to touch them and try them on. Then they served me tea.

The woman who seemed to be in charge began. "We know that you were born in Kiev, and you came back in hopes of finding your parents. We understand that, and there is something we can do for you. Tomorrow your group leaves here. Do you have a partner, a roommate, on this trip?"

"Yes."

"Well, when it is time to board the bus, stay in your room. When she leaves, lock the door and stay here where you belong. You were born here and you belong here."

"No. I am an American citizen now."

"We will find your family for you. If you want, the local TV station can run two minutes with you talking. You can give the names of the people you are looking for. If you have pictures, they will show them. It may help you find your family. It will only cost you $7,000 USD." (approximately 465,000 rubles).

I didn't have the money to give them to do that, and I had no reason to believe they would be honest with my money. And saddest of all, I had no pictures. Mama had sewn pictures into the lining of our coats, but everything was gone. So I left Kiev the next day.

A bus driver told me there were two archives in the city. I didn't find anything in the first archive. The second one I was unable to locate in the time that was given to me. Everyone acted like Kopytina was not a real name. I left there without learning anything. It was all so very disappointing.

Return to Russia, 1988

By 1988, the Communists were no longer in charge, and Americans could travel more freely. I hoped that now I could get more information about my parents.

I took my 29-year-old daughter along with me. In all fairness to Renee, you need to know that my children knew nothing about my past except that I was born in Russia and survived the war. I wasn't ready to talk if they had asked me. When they were children, then teenagers, and later getting on with their own lives as young, independent people, they didn't ask.

Growing up in America, Renee had no way to understand my past until she actually experienced it in Russia. She saw that even the nicest hotels there would not earn even the lowest ratings in America. The nicest restaurants had only one thing to offer, and that was usually a potato dish. She had come on this trip to be with me, but she had also left her small children at home. I knew she was ready to go back to the United States. That was completely understandable. This was my second search for information on my parents. I was disappointed and saddened to come home with nothing more.

1993, Lena Karnova

In 1993, Lena Karnova was teaching Russian at George Fox University in Newberg, Oregon. My pastor knew about her and asked me if I would get her and show her around Portland. I was happy to do so. She was around 35 years old.

I brought her to my house, which is modest—but grand by Russian standards. I took her to the Country Kitchen buffet where it seemed there was no end to the choices of food one could have. She wanted to go shopping, so we went to moderately priced stores where, again, the choices and prices were almost too much to take in.

She had a small room at the university, and I helped her set it up with curtains and things like that. As we spent a good deal of time in the car, I began to tell her my story. Some of the history of Russia and its people she had never heard. There still was a great fear in Russia to talk about the past. There had been so much fear, pain, and suffering over the years. Younger people didn't know the stories hiding inside their elders.

Lena cried easily, just like I do, as I told her my story. I talked, and we both would cry. Sometimes, I had to find a place to pull the car over so we could cry together. I told her I wanted information on my family more than anything. Lena asked what I expected to get since both my mother and father were dead. I told her I had an aunt and uncle. I was sure my grandmother was dead because of her condition the last time I had seen her.

I told her that more than anything, I wished for a picture of my mama and papa. I was beginning to lose an image in my mind of Mama's smile and of the way Papa would walk, clasping his hands behind his back when he was thinking. I never forgot that they were such a handsome couple, but I wasn't sure I remembered the way they actually looked. Was it just my dreams or reality? I told her these things, but I knew it was too late and impossible.

Lena told me that she had some connections and she might be able to find somebody, but she could not talk about it. Maybe she could help me locate at least one person. That might get it started. She told me to write down every name and place that I could give her. She wanted my e-mail address.

"Lena, I don't have e-mail, and I don't know about it and how to use it." So I asked Doctor Nielsen if I could use the e-mail at work, and he said I could. I gave her names of all my family. I didn't expect much. And to tell you the truth, I didn't even think much about it.

On my trip to Russia in 1979, I was contacted at the hotel by a television person. She said that she knew I was looking for family, and she could put my picture on TV. The cost would be only $7,000 USD; that was just too much money for me to pay. But she kept on trying to persuade me to do it. "Someone is likely to see you and recognize you and your family name, and they will be able to contact you." Still, I couldn't see paying that. First, I didn't have it. Second, it wouldn't bring my parents back. It would only possibly give me some information.

So I gave Lena every name I could think of, and mostly, I just forgot about it. About 3 months later, on Tuesday, January 11, 1994, I was home when the doctor's office called to tell me that there was an e-mail to me, and it was in Russian. My heart felt like it stopped beating. I had given up on getting any news of my parents. Was there any? I got to the office as fast as I could.

Doctor Nielsen and staff were eager to hear. I read, *"We have found much information about your family, and we even have pictures."* I was about to faint. I was unsure of this news. I had to be strong. I had to not wish for too much. Maybe she had the wrong family. Maybe her information wasn't correct. So I rushed home and called her in Russia.

"Lena, there has to be a mistake. How can you have pictures? Mine were lost in Auschwitz, and Mama was thrown off that train and died."

"Someone saved her, Valia. She didn't die. And your father didn't die, either. They are both dead now, but they made it back and found each other."

How can I even begin to describe that moment? Joy? Joy that they made it back and found each other? Sadness? I was sad beyond words that we never found one another and that they never knew what happened to their only child. I physically hurt. I hurt in a way that I could only now understand as a mother myself.

I knew the unbelievable pain of a parent when a child dies. I had experienced that. But to be a parent who lived never knowing what happened? How did they live not knowing? I still wasn't sure I could believe this new information. I had so long believed they were dead.

I asked her to describe the pictures to me, and as she did, the shell of disbelief began to crack, and I gradually came to believe she really did have pictures of my mama and papa and me. Can you imagine? It had been 62 years! I would give up every possession I now had for one picture of them.

"I'm going to come to get them. I'll be there as soon as I can. Maybe tonight or tomorrow."

"No, Valia. It is not necessary. Someone very important that I know is flying to New York tomorrow and will hand carry them."

"Then I will meet him in New York."

"Hold on. Wait. I will have this comrade call you when he gets to New York."

I couldn't sleep for fear he would lose those pictures or not call me. But the next day, he called me and said, "I have your pictures."

"I will fly there to get them. Where are you?"

"No. It won't be necessary. I have been assured there is a delivery system here that will have them at your house tomorrow morning."

"Can I pay?"

"Absolutely not."

The next day, my husband was out golfing when there was a knock on the door. I was home alone. Can you place yourself in that moment? Can you even *imagine* it? A delivery person handed me the package. I held it in my arms. I just held it and held it, but I could not open it. I called my friend Betty and told her what I was going through. Then I called my daughter Renee and told her.

"Mama, I'll be right over."

When they each arrived, we sat on the couch together. So much fear and excitement mixed up inside me. I was nauseated, but I could no longer wait. I opened the package.

There they were. I looked into the faces of my mama, papa, and me, and I started screaming. The pain and joy came from so far away and so deep inside me. I jumped up, holding those pictures, and ran screaming into the kitchen. Renee caught me just before I fell. It was like they had come back to me from the grave. I could see them again, and in seeing, I remembered. I remembered their touch, their smell, their love, their joy and fear.

Lena had told me on the phone that Mama had died at age 52, and Papa had just died 3 years before at age 90. We had been so close during my visits when I tried to find them.

Lena had also told me on the phone that my father had remarried after Mama died. The woman's name was Taicia. She and her husband lived across the hall from Mama and Papa, and Taicia was Mama's friend. Taicia's husband died, and sometime after Mama died, she and Papa married. Taicia had two children. It took me through the winter to calm down from all the news and take it in, but after I did, I wanted to face Kiev and meet Taicia, and learn whatever she could tell me.

In the meantime, Doctor Nielsen took pictures of my small, old, worn pictures and then had those developed into the large pictures that I have framed. Those I keep hanging in my art room. I would not let anyone else have the originals. I would not let them out of my possession.

Return to Russia, April 1994

The same day I got those pictures, I knew I had to go to Russia again. But it was winter. It was too cold there. I knew I needed to let all this new information sink into me. I was grieving again but in a new way. Now, I knew for sure that Papa and Mama were dead. There was no more hope. I had to let all my feelings settle. I was finally ready to go about 3 months later, in the spring. I had talked several times on the phone with Lena. She helped to prepare me for my visit. Taicia knew I was coming as well as her daughter, Tamara, who was about 10 years younger than me.

Lena and the university president met me at the airport when I arrived and gave me a bouquet of lilies of the valley. It was Mama's favorite flower. They decided that I would stay at the president's house the first night. Early in the morning, she went to work. I woke up rested and looked around and saw a mess. Messy, messy, and so cluttered. I couldn't move around or sit without papers, books, clothes, and just general stuff in the way. I didn't feel comfortable moving her things. She was gone to work, and I was left all alone, feeling very uncomfortable.

I finally decided to use her phone and called Taicia and told her how I felt. I will try this in Russian, "*skuchno.*" I am trying to say "claustrophobic."

"I need to get out of here."

Taicia said, "Come to our place to stay. Come now."

I had her address, and somebody came to pick me up. I don't remember how I got there. She lived in an apartment with her daughter, Tamara. When I walked in, it was spotlessly clean and organized. That alone helped me to feel more comfortable. I didn't feel excitement about meeting them. It really was more like sadness that I felt. I told myself, "She is not my mother, but she is nice, and I can warm up to her."

It turned out that Taicia couldn't tell me very much. Papa wouldn't talk. It still wasn't safe to talk. Imagine a society with so much fear and distrust built into it that you don't talk to your own family. Your own spouse. She told me things like, "Your papa always wanted a carefully ironed white shirt to wear to work. Your mama waited on him hand and foot. When we got married, I had to teach him to do some things for himself."

She said that hundreds of his men survived the war and the prison. Over the years, they would all gather at the beach and talk and remember. They held him in the greatest respect. They called him, "Our

Leader," but learned not to say that in public places as it was not safe.

She told me that he always liked to drink his tea from a certain cup, and she gave the cup to me. She told me how much he loved my mama. That night, she insisted that I take her bed, and she slept on the couch.

The next day, I wanted to visit the cemeteries where my parents were buried. They knew the cemetery that Mama was buried in and how to get there, so we took a bus. I wanted to go. I had to go. But I didn't want to go and wasn't sure I really could because it would make it all so final.

We arrived at an old cemetery with many trees, and the ground was covered in weeds and tall grass. It was so overgrown and unkempt. The ornate iron gates to the cemetery were open. I was already crying before we found anything. I couldn't seem to stop. Another woman came to see what was going on and said she would take care of this. We told her the year Mama died, and she pointed in a direction where she would likely be buried. It was a difficult search. We searched for hours. I was running through bushes and weeds and came to a small area surrounded by a wrought iron fence. I opened the gate to get inside and saw a space planned for two people to be buried. Mama was on one side, and there was the space where Papa was supposed to be buried, but he died in a year the cemetery was closed, so he could not be buried there.

Her headstone was large and supposed to be white, but it was covered in dirt and moss. It had once had a big iron cross on it, but that had been ripped off. Papa had inscribed on the stone . . . I'll have to translate: "TO MY WIFE MOST LOVED," Nadeschda 1905–1957. When I read that, I lost all strength in my body and mind. I had an impulse to get on the ground and crawl around and dig with my hands . . . dig and dig to get her out, to hug her, to say the good-bye we never got to say, to tell her what had happened and let her know I made it. I wanted to scream, "I'm OK, Mama." I didn't do that, of course, but the desire was exploding inside me.

There was a spot inside the gated area that had a little stone bench large enough for one person to sit on. "Your papa would come here often and visit," Taicia told me. I sat on that bench where my father had sat so often. I looked up. Trees covered the area. I could see blue sky through the branches. Birds were making so many sounds. It was springtime. They were probably nesting. Getting ready for new life. I thought, "This is good, Mama. Looking up, this is real pretty. You would like it."

I paid some people well who agreed to clean up the grave site and replace the cross and repair and paint the fence. I was so exhausted I asked if they would just get a cab to take us home. I paid for everything, of course. People in Russia had so little money.

The next day, I wanted to go where Papa was buried. He had already paid for that place where Mama was, and burial in Russia is so expensive. Maybe that was why he was cremated. I have a hard time with that after my experiences in Auschwitz. His ashes are in a small space in a wall that is outside.

Taicia began to tell me more about Papa. He became a bad diabetic about age 82, and he started going blind. He had a lot of trouble walking because he would lose his balance. He died at home with Taicia at his side. Many people came and told her that they had very seldom seen such a spotless house and body. The family cleaned the body and dressed it and laid it out on a table in their home. People came by the house to pay their respect. The next day, the person would be buried, or, in this case, cremated.

In the time I was there, I came to love Tamara. We did so much laughing and crying together. Papa was good to her. We still call each other. I wish I could see her more.

Lena's Driver

Lena had her driver come to pick me up one day. I asked the driver, "Where is Lena?"

"At home."

"Does she drive?"

"No."

The driver took me to the building where she lived, a building which is five or six stories high and very beautiful. He walked me to the front door and told me she was on the third floor. I went in alone, and he returned to the car. I rang the bell and was let inside. This was luxurious! There was a large, beautiful kitchen and a refrigerator. "Where does all this come from?" is all I could think. This is not the Russia I have seen here and always known.

She greeted me so nice and friendly. "See my new home. When I saw your house, I loved it. I copied some of your things, like the glass cupboards showing the dishes. I love this place."

I was stunned. She asked me to go with her to their summer house. She served me some refreshments. Soon, a van came to get us. It was big enough for at least eight people, and it was shiny and new.

"Is that yours?"

"Yes."

"Where is your husband?"

"He is busy and is out of town quite a bit with his job. He buys coal for Kiev."

When the driver took me home, I asked a lot of questions and learned that the drivers were not getting paid. Some had not been paid for 6 months!

"Why do you keep working then?"

"Because maybe someday we will be paid, and there is nothing else to do."

That ended my relationship with Lena. I couldn't continue it. I never actually told her why. I knew that she would know, and she never tried to contact me again either.

The House (of God), December 2008

"Oh, Glenda, Glenda. I'm so glad you came." She was bouncing up and down, all five feet of her, with sparkling, clear blue eyes, and a smile about to jump off her face, she was so excited.

"This morning about 7:30, my phone rang. A woman was talking so clearly, that it could have been you.

"The woman asked, 'Is this Valentina Michauloina Kopytina?' and I thought, 'Who is this woman? I know that name.'

"That was so crazy, but see, in Russia, they would call me by my complete first name and my father's last name. You do that out of respect. I knew that name was familiar, but I don't hear it anymore.

"I was so excited and trying to talk fast so we wouldn't run out of time, but she kept telling me to slow down. And the connection was so clear. I couldn't believe how clear it was.

"You remember I told you that for many years I sent all those boxes and boxes of clothes and food to Russia? Well, the caller was the woman I sent them to in a little village. I don't remember the name of the village right now. It was just a small place in the country. Not like the big city of Kiev where I had lived.

"Well, in about 1996, I was visiting in Kiev, and I wanted to take a ride into the country. We came to a little village. It looked like a poor place. I wanted to get out and take a walk. I was walking through the little street looking at the houses when I saw this field. I still remember that field because it was so green. I remember thinking that the grass in my yard in the United States is not that green. In that field was something like hay bales, and out in the distance beyond one hill was another little hill. But the hill was big enough to put a house on it. You might have to take some of the top off it to make it flatter, but you would be able to build a house on it and see so much from up there. You could see that beautiful green field all around you, and you could probably see more things in the distance. When I got back to where I was staying, to the same place where I later sent all those boxes, I told them about how pretty that place was.

"Anyway, today on the phone, she told me, 'Valentina, remember that hill? Well, we have a house on it now.' ("House" is the word for church.)

"Here is how we built it. Remember all those clothes and food and money you would send to us? Well, we would tell the people, 'Come help us build this house (church), and you can have a meal and get some clothes.' The men built, and the women cooked, and everyone got clothes and food. And that is how it got built. Now, every time we meet, we thank God for this House and for Valentina who helped us build this house.

"And, Valentina, we have the key. We have the key to the house."

In the context of Communism, when no one owned anything, having the "key to the house" meant ownership—a pride and joy that you cannot imagine if you were raised in the U.S.

"I never imagined anything beyond food and clothing could happen. I would send about 10 boxes a month. I would pay $10 per box for postage, and The Nazarene Mission in Portland would come and pick them up and pay the rest to send them. I kept very good records. I sent 1,557 boxes. I bought everything to put in there, and I packed them myself. I would put a number inside each box, and this woman in Russia that got the boxes would write me back and tell me which boxes had arrived, and I would mark them off in my book. That way, I knew everything arrived at the right place.

"I finally had to quit when I stopped working and because my back was beginning to be a problem from all the lifting.

"Can you believe they used those gifts to get the help to build a church? And she told me recently they took up a collection of money too so they could call and tell me about it."

Valentina Michailovna Kopytina, known to us as Vallie, your generosity, compassion, love, talent, and skills have touched the lives of all who have had the privilege of knowing you and countless others who only knew your name as:

Valentina, Valia, Lidia, Vallie . . .

CPSIA information can be obtained
at www.ICGtesting.com
Printed in the USA
FFHW020641130319
51036083-56448FF